Come Away With Me is a prophetic meditation on the Song of Solomon (based on the New King James Version where the Shulamite, representing the Bride of Christ, and the Beloved, representing the Lord Jesus, discuss the meaning of the song.

This meditation was received through 'journalling'. That is, the author asked the Lord to talk to him about the Song of Solomon and then wrote down the thoughts that came into his mind. It should be remembered that we prophesy in part and that all prophecy should be judged. 1 Cor 13:9, 14:29.

Come Away with Me

A Prophetic Meditation on the Song of Solomon

JONATHAN HINDSLEY

NATHANAEL BOOKS
Burnley

Copyright © Jonathan Hindsley 2003

First published 2003

Published by Nathanael Books
c/o 27 Mosedale Drive, Burnley
Lancashire BB12 8UJ.

ISBN 0 9545286 0 3

Book design and production for the publisher by
Bookprint Creative Services, P.O. Box 827,
BN21 3YJ, England.
Printed in Great Britain.

To Marilyn
My companion and the wife of my youth
with whom I live joyfully all the days of my life

CONTENTS

FOREWORD

Come Away With Me is a striking example of a new style of book which, I believe, will begin sweeping the earth – books that couple the revelation of the Holy Spirit today with yesterday's revelation by the Holy Spirit as recorded for us in the Bible, the Word of God.

The exciting rediscovery of the twentieth century was that God is still speaking with man, and we can still hear Him. This book is a fascinating illustration of this dynamic, as Jonathan Hindsley goes verse by verse with God through the Song of Solomon, asking God questions about the text he is reading, and recording God's responses to him.

Now, we believe that the current words of God need to be in agreement with those things God has already spoken to us in the Holy Scriptures, which we consider to be fully accurate and completely infallible. Thus, every word of God today will and must be tested against the words God has spoken to us in the Holy Bible.

Paul prays in Ephesians 1:17,18 'that the God of our Lord Jesus Christ, the Father of glory, may give to you a spirit of wisdom and of revelation in the knowledge of

Him. I pray that the eyes of your heart may be enlightened, so that you will know what is the hope of His calling, what are the riches of the glory of His inheritance in the saints' (NASU). This prayer is for us as readers of the Word of God to receive fresh revelation concerning the things we are reading about in the Bible. David prayed the same prayer in Psalm 119:18 when he said, 'Open my eyes, that I may behold wonderful things from Your law' (NASU).

Jonathan Hindsley has prayed these prayers and then recorded for the reader what God has revealed to him. Now the reader can be blessed by the testimony of Jonathan's interaction with God as he takes us through the Song of Songs. I pray you find this a great blessing as you prayerfully read over Jonathan's prophetic meditation on the Song of Solomon.

Dr. Mark Virkler –
President of Christian Leadership University
Author of *Communion With God*

AUTHOR'S NOTE

In May 2000 I attended a conference at Revival Fires, Dudley, England when I heard Mark Virkler teach on 'communion with God'. He introduced me to the idea that it was possible to tune to the flow of the Holy Spirit and write down what God was saying. As a 'left brainer' I thought at first that this was not for me, but I decided to have a go anyway. To begin with I struggled a bit but then found to my surprise that I did start hearing from the Lord. After the weekend I continued to experiment with 'journalling' and one day opened my Bible at the Song of Solomon. I decided to ask the Lord the question, 'Can You explain what it means for You to kiss me with the kisses of Your mouth?' The answer was the beginning of this book.

I would like to extend my thanks to Mark Virkler of Communion With God Ministries for teaching me how to 'tune to flow' and hear from God. Without his teaching this book would not have happened. I would also like to thank Sharon and Trevor Baker of Revival Fires for providing a well of refreshing at the Grace Centre, Dudley.

Mark Virkler can be contacted via
<www.cwgministries.org> and likewise Revival Fires
via <www.revivalfires.org.uk>.

Song of Solomon

CHAPTER ONE

Song 1:1–2

BRIDE   *Lord, I can understand a woman saying 'let Him kiss me with the kisses of His mouth', but for a man this is a little difficult. Can you explain what it means for You to kiss me with the kisses of Your mouth?*

JESUS   Loving-kindness, affection, to pour out blessing on you, to blow gently on you with the breeze of My Spirit, to whisper My word into your heart, to spend time together. It's the intimacy of My Spirit joined to your spirit.[1] It's the warmth of My love for you, My embrace, for your love is better than wine to Me. I long for that intimate relationship, just being together. I long for you to spend time with Me. Your kisses are worship.[2] That intoxicates Me more than wine. Put your head on My breast and rest there like John.[3] You are safe in My arms.

BRIDE   *Lord, why is love better than wine?*

JESUS   Your love intoxicates Me, gives Me a warm

13

s My reward. There is no hangover
forever. It is eternal. It is what I died
great reward.[4]

.hat is loving-kindness?

ıo the little things for you that you want Me to
ɔ bless you. I delight in giving you pleasure, in
blessing you and meeting your needs.[5] Nothing is too
hard for Me.[6] I would withhold nothing from you.[7] I
love you, and My desire is to bless you. The mercies of
the Lord (or loving-kindness) endure forever.[8]

BRIDE *Can You explain a bit more about blowing gently with
the breeze of Your Spirit?*

JESUS My voice coming gently, whispering in your ear.[9]
Learn to recognise that voice. You will need to be able
to hear Me.[10] The wind of the Spirit takes what I say
and gives it to you.[11] Be sensitive and still and you will
hear Me. The Spirit is My breath.[12] The Spirit is My
life.[13] I breathed into Adam and he became a life-
giving spirit.[14]

BRIDE *What do You mean – a life-giving spirit?*

JESUS He had the potential to pass that life on to all
humanity. So do you as a new adam.[15]

BRIDE *You said that my kisses are worship. Can You explain
that a bit more?*

JESUS Yes. When you worship Me it's as though you
kissed Me. Praise is different. I enjoy your praise, but
your worship really turns Me on. That is My reward.
That's what made it all worthwhile, the promise of
those intimate moments with you in worship. Our
hearts beating together as one.[16] That's when you kiss
Me and I love it. That's the joy that was set before Me.
I had My eyes fixed on you when I went to the cross,

and it was all worth it. I long for the moments when My Bride spends time with Me in sweet embrace.

Song 1:3–4

BRIDE *Lord, what do You mean by the fragrance of Your good ointments?*

JESUS I am the Balm of Gilead,[17] I am the Rose of Sharon.[18] I am the anointing oil that runs down the beard of Aaron and brings unity.[19] That oil was specially perfumed.[20] Unity is a sweet perfume to Me. My Spirit brings life and healing wherever He goes.[21] He brings a sweet smell to all that is putrid and diseased. My name is as ointment poured forth on all the disease (dis-ease) of the world. My good ointments are the fruit of the Spirit: love, joy, peace, patience, kindness, goodness, faithfulness, gentleness and self control.[22] This is what the world needs, and if only they would turn to Me I would heal their hurts. I am the Great Physician.[23] There is healing in My name. I bore their sorrows, their pains and their sicknesses and by My stripes they are healed.[24] If only they knew it. But so many want to remain in their filth and rottenness. This is a foul smell in My nostrils. I want to heal their hurts and pour ointment on their wounds. My ointments are good and have a sweet fragrance.

BRIDE *Lord, why do the virgins love You?*

JESUS The virgins are those who are pure of heart. They shall see God, and that is why they love Me.[25] They have been healed and purified by My ointment and they are a sweet smelling fragrance to My Father –

and so are you.[26] I love you, My Bride.

BRIDE *Lead me away, Lord.*

JESUS Yes, let's go somewhere quiet. If you will spend time with Me I will show you many things. As we are quiet together I can talk to you.

BRIDE *The daughters of Jerusalem will run after us.*

JESUS (Chuckle) Yes, they will. Let them come for they desire My presence. But I can still have time alone with you – if you will let Me. I want to develop this time together. I am opening up a whole new element in our relationship. It is precious and of great value.

BRIDE *'The King has brought me into His chambers'. Where is Your chamber, Lord?*

JESUS My chamber is the still place where we can be alone together. I want to spend more time there with you. My chamber is the secret place, your heart. Enthrone Me in your heart. Let Me be king.

BRIDE *Tell me more about the secret place, the chamber.*

JESUS The chamber of your heart is the intimate place where My Spirit dwells.[27] It is through the Spirit that I fellowship with you.

BRIDE *Lord, if Your chamber is my heart, then how have You brought me into that place?*

JESUS I have drawn you. I have brought you to the place where you have given Me your heart to be My chamber. I have wooed you and brought you to the place of intimacy. That is My goal and My desire. I am so glad you have come. Come, let us share the cup together, the cup of the covenant.[28]

BRIDE *Who are the daughters of Jerusalem and why do they rejoice in me?*

JESUS They rejoice in you because you have found

favour with Me. The daughters are all your brothers and sisters. They are also My Bride. This is a mystery. I love each of you individually and all of you together as one. Each one of you is precious in My eyes, each one of you is My Bride as an individual, and together you are My Bride. That is why I prayed for you to be one, as I and My Father are one.[16] This is why the daughters will also remember My love more than wine.

BRIDE   *They are right to love You, Jesus. You are so precious to us. You are our life, our very being.*

Song 1:5–6

JESUS   You are dark and you are lovely. The darkness is a beauty of the inner being.

BRIDE   *Lord, can You explain what You mean by that.*

JESUS   I mean that the dark night of the soul has been turned into beauty. Beauty for ashes.[29] The tents of Kedar (*Bedouin tents made out of black goatskin.*) are made from dark skins. They are dark inside. Until a lamp is lit nothing can be seen. The interior is dark and gloomy. Your soul was dark and gloomy before the light of My presence illumined it.[30] I have put My light within you and now your beauty shines forth for all to see.[31] Your brothers were jealous of you for your relationship with Me and they put you to work. Expect some persecution[32], particularly from other more carnal believers, when you come close to Me. They will resent the special relationship that we have and will seek to destroy it. But look after your vineyard, My love. Your vineyard is your relationship with Me. It is so precious. Let nothing get in the way.

Song 1:7

BRIDE *Where do You make Your flock rest at noon? And where do You feed Your flock?*

JESUS I make My flock rest in the green pastures, by the still waters, for I am their shepherd, and I am a good shepherd.[33] I guard My flock for they are precious to Me, and to My Father. I love My Father and therefore I love His flock. I will guard and protect them with My life. I have already done that.

BRIDE *Where are the green pastures and still waters?*

JESUS In quietness and confidence is your strength.[34] Strength comes from food. Food is My word.[35] As you digest and meditate on My word you build up your spirit. The quiet places, the still waters, are the times you spend with Me, allowing My Spirit to speak to you like this. Noon is the heat of the day and the time to rest. In the midst of life's hustle and bustle, at the busiest times, you must take time out to rest and be with Me. I make My sheep lie down in green pastures, beside still waters, and I talk to them. That is when they learn to recognise My voice. If My sheep will not be still and listen they will not learn to hear My voice.

BRIDE *Why should I veil myself?*

JESUS You should not veil yourself. You should shine forth. Let everyone see your beauty, for you are beautiful indeed. It is your inner beauty, that beauty that is hidden in the tents of Kedar that has now been illumined by My Spirit. Put the lamp on a hill. Don't hide it under a bushel. Shine forth My precious one, and let the world see what I have done in you.[36] That will attract them to Me so that I can do the same for them. Take the veil off. Don't be ashamed of who and what I have made you. You are so beautiful. You have no idea how beautiful you are, My love.

Song 1:8

BRIDE   *Who, or what, are my little goats, Lord?*

JESUS   Follow the flocks. Follow the shepherd who leads the flocks. Stay with Me and I will give you goats, and they will be as sheep. Feed them My word and they too will be My sheep. You turn a goat into a sheep by feeding it the right food – My word. Goats are rebellious and 'butt' at everything, but as they feed on My word My word changes them, and as they stop arguing and butting and submit, they become sheep. Then they can hear My voice. You cannot hear My voice if you keep arguing with Me. Feed the goats I give you. Let them mix with the sheep and I will change them into sheep.

Song 1:9

BRIDE   *Lord, why have You compared me to one of Pharaoh's fillies?*

JESUS   Not to one of Pharaoh's fillies – to My filly among Pharaoh's chariots. My filly is beautiful. Pharaoh's chariots are in the world, they are the world system. You are My filly in the world. Horses are strong. You are strong and you will work for Me in the world.

Song 1:10

BRIDE   *What are the ornaments on my cheeks and neck?*

JESUS   The ornaments you wear are the gifts I have given you. When you came to Me you had no beauty of your own. But I have adorned you with My gifts. My gifts that I have given you are the fruit of the Spirit.[22] Your adornments are on the inside making your darkness lovely.[37] It is that inner beauty that will attract people to Me, when they see what I can do for them, as they look on you. The gold is My glory that I am about to adorn My bride with. I will place My glory round your neck as a chain of office to tell the world you have My authority[38] and you are Mine.

Song 1:11

BRIDE   *Why would the daughters want to make me ornaments?*

JESUS   Beware of counterfeit ornaments. The church will try to copy the ornaments I will give you. They will try to make you beautiful their way, by rules and regulations, by religion. This is not true beauty. It does not attract Me. My bride, make sure that only My ornaments adorn you. Do not be deceived. Only what I give you will stand the test. Only what I give you will attract the world to Me. Those in the world will recognise the counterfeit. They are searching for Me, and as you wear My ornaments, that come by My Spirit working in you, they will see Me. Be warned – religion will try to corrupt you. True beauty comes by a pure heart and a right spirit within you. These are

My ornaments and these are what I want you to wear.

Songs 1:12

BRIDE   *What is my spikenard?*

JESUS   Your spikenard is your perfume. Your perfume is a sweet smelling fragrance that endears Me to you. Your perfume comes to Me in a quiet, gentle, submissive spirit. I love it when you submit to Me and flow with Me. Remember that unity is like the precious oil that flows down the beard of Aaron. That's not just talking about unity amongst believers. It also speaks of unity between Me and My bride. That anointing oil was specially perfumed, and as you lie with Me, by My side, in unity with Me, then that fragrance rises to My nostrils and blesses Me.

Song 1:13–14

BRIDE   *Lord, will You explain verses 13 and 14*

JESUS   Don't you know what that means? Think about it. You can use your mind as you meditate My word.

BRIDE   *Yes Lord, you are a sweet smelling fragrance to me. All that is out there in the world is a stench compared with the fragrance that comes from You. You are precious to me and I love You Lord. You are a sweet smelling fragrance to me too; precious ointment that heals my hurts. You are the balm of Gilead.[17] You are all that is beautiful to me. Nothing else compares with You.*

Song 1:15

JESUS   You are fair My love. You are fair. You see you are
no longer dark, but now you are fair. The light of My
presence within you has transformed you completely.
What was dark through the burning of the sun has
become fair through the burning of the Son. I have
purified you by fire, and as I continue to purify you,
you will become fairer and fairer, and purer and
purer.[39] As you become pure, more and more pure,
you become more and more transparent. The more
transparent you become the more My glory can shine
out of you.[40] You have dove's eyes. The dove is a
symbol of My Spirit.[41] You have the eyes of My Spirit –
gentleness and peace, and you can see clearly.

Song 1:16–17

BRIDE   *What does it mean by our bed being green?*
JESUS   We lie in pleasant places together. We have the
best. Am I handsome? Do you love Me?
BRIDE   *Yes Jesus, there is none to compare with You and I do
love You.*

Song
of
Solomon

CHAPTER TWO

Song 2:1

BRIDE   *Lord, there appears to be some confusion over who is the rose of Sharon. You are usually referred to as the Rose of Sharon but the scripture seems to indicate that the bride is the rose of Sharon. Which is correct?*

JESUS   You are indeed the rose of Sharon and the lily of the valley.

BRIDE   *Then why did You say You were the Rose of Sharon earlier when we talked about the fragrance of Your good ointments?*

JESUS   You and I are one. If you are the rose of Sharon then so am I. It doesn't really matter. Don't get bogged down with technicalities. You are the rose of peace – Sharon means peace. I am the Prince of Peace.[1] We are one.

BRIDE   *What are You saying, Lord, about the rose?*

JESUS   You are the rose of Sharon, the lily of the valley. Out of the plain, the smooth place, the fruitful place,

23

the peaceful place, grows a beautiful flower. I am that plain. I am the fruitful place. I am the fertile place, the peaceful place. As you abide in Me then you shall grow into a beautiful flower. You will blossom and be a delight to all around you. As the rain of My Spirit falls on you the flower springs up and opens up. Let My Spirit water you as you rest in the valley, in the quiet still place that is in Me. You have been planted. You abide in the fertile soil and God will give the increase. He will cause you to flower and be beautiful. I am that fertile soil. Abide in Me and let My word abide in you.[2] Do not always seek the mountain tops. Mountain top experiences are good. You get a clear view from the heights, but it is in the valley, on the plain where all is smooth, that the real growth occurs. That is where the water is. That is where there is peace and tranquillity, and that is where growth occurs. It may seem that in the valley nothing much is happening, and you can't see far, but it is there, as you abide in Me, that I cause you to grow and blossom. Suddenly you are a flower, beautiful for all to see. Don't despise the valley, the smooth place, for that is the fruitful place, where the water of My Spirit[3] flows into you and refreshes you causing you to grow and blossom.

Song 2:2

BRIDE　*Why am I like a lily among thorns?*

JESUS　You are special to Me. You stand out from the others. Each one of you who are My bride is special to Me. You are all individuals and each is as important as the other.[4] Do not look down on yourselves and think 'Oh I am not as special as that person' or 'Jesus loves that one more than me'. No, I love each of you equally. You are special to Me. You stand out from the others. You are a lily among thorns. In My eyes that is how I see you. You are a special treasure to Me,[5] a lily among thorns.

Song 2:3

BRIDE   *Why are You like an apple tree, Lord?*

JESUS   The apple tree bears good fruit. Many trees do not bear fruit, but the apple does. It speaks of being the focus of the Father's attention. I am special to Him and I bear good fruit. You are the good fruit that I have borne. You are the result of the work I did on the cross. Out of that work has come good fruit that is a delight to Me and My Father. Sit in My shade and spend time with Me and delight in Me.

BRIDE   *What do You mean – Your fruit is sweet to my mouth?*

JESUS   Do not be misled by Satan's lie about the tree of the knowledge of good and evil.[6] That was not an apple tree. I am the apple tree and My fruit is good. Taste of My fruit and you will see that it is good.[7] Everything I give you is good. Only good gifts come from the Father.[8] Rejoice in Me. O taste and see that the Lord is good. There is no knowledge of evil in Me, only what is good and pure and of good report.[9]

Song 2:4

BRIDE   *Talk to me about Your banqueting house.*

JESUS   I have so much to give you. Come and feast on Me. Let Me satisfy you with the new wine of My presence. Do not be drunk with natural wine in which is dissipation but be drunk with the new wine of My Spirit.[10] Be continually filled with the new wine. You cannot have too much of My Spirit. Let the new wine flow in you and through you so that it blesses others also. In My banqueting house there is much wine. This new wine will never run dry. This is the best wine that I served at Cana.[11] That was a picture of My kingdom. The bridegroom was trying to supply the needs of the people through natural means. The world cannot supply what you need. But I supplied a foretaste of the new wine of the kingdom. That is why the guests thought he had saved the best until last. I do not want you to get drunk on natural wine when I have provided super-natural wine instead. Come to My banqueting house and drink the wine that I supply – the wine of My Spirit. Let Me fill you. Let Me intoxicate you with My love. Once you have truly tasted the wine of My love, you will never want the world's wine again.

BRIDE   *Lord, You said that Your banner over me is love. What is Your banner?*

JESUS   My banner is My protection. It is a covering stretched out over you – a canopy to keep the sun from scorching you. My love is stretched out over you to provide protection from the heat of the world. With a canopy of My love stretched out over you nothing, and no-one, can harm you.[12] Sit under the shade of My banner and feast with Me.

Song 2:5

BRIDE *Why do I need to be sustained with cakes of raisins and apples?*

JESUS You are lovesick. Once you have tasted My love, truly tasted it, you will never be satisfied. You will always hunger for more of Me. Nothing else will satisfy but My presence.[13] I am the apple tree. The apple is My fruit. Raisins are from the fruit of the vine. I am the vine.[14] From the fruit of the vine comes the new wine. The cakes of raisins and the apples speak of Me. You are lovesick for Me. You hunger for My love and only I can satisfy you, only I can refresh you.

Song 2:6

BRIDE *Your left hand is under my head and Your right hand embraces me.*

JESUS Yes, as you lie by My side I cradle your head and I embrace you. As I hold you in My arms you are secure. No one can snatch you out of My arms.[15] In the intimate place with Me there is security, there is comfort, there is love and there is acceptance.[16] Come to Me and lie with Me that I might enfold you with My arms and love you. My desire is for you to be close to Me. Oh how I ache for you, how I long for you, My lover and My bride.[17] You will never know how much I desire you. You are My reward and I want to be with you. These intimate moments are so precious to Me. Come away with Me, My love, My bride, My fair one. You are no longer dark. There is no darkness in you now. Yes, you are beautiful, you are fair, you are filled with the light of My presence and My presence shines forth out of you so that you can be a light to the world. This is the product of the intimacy we share. It is the product of our love. Therefore spend time with Me. There are many others that must be a part of My bride and it is our love that will attract them. So spend time with Me and love Me. Come into the intimate place My love and let Me hold you.

Song 2:7

BRIDE *What does verse seven mean, Lord? Why should the daughters not stir up love until it pleases?*

JESUS Love for Me will become a consuming fire in you. My love is not something you can trifle with or take lightly. If you say 'yes' to Me it will consume your whole life.[18] I will not awaken love in you until you give Me permission, but believe Me, when you do say 'yes' to Me things will never be the same again. You will never be able to go back to what was.[19] Once you have tasted the new wine of My love the old will never satisfy. Be warned, you will be 'ruined'. Religion will not satisfy, the world will not satisfy, for when love is awakened in you it will cry out for Me. You will become love sick for Me and only I will satisfy. Do you want to be like this? Do you really want this? Do you want a passion, a consuming fire burning within you? Think carefully. No, do not think. If your heart, your soul, your spirit cries out 'yes' then say 'yes', and I will come and awaken love in you. But that is why I warn the daughters of Jerusalem not to awaken love until it pleases, for there will be no going back to that which was before.

Song 2:8

BRIDE *Lord, why do You come leaping on the mountains?*

JESUS My bride was listening for My voice. She was longing to hear My voice and instantly recognised it when I called out.[20] Do you, My church, My bride, recognise My voice? Are you listening for My voice? Do you rejoice when you hear Me speak? Are you longing to hear Me? My bride is listening and is eager for Me to come. I will come bounding over the hills, leaping and running to be with the one I love. Nothing will keep Me from My bride, My love, My fair one.

Song 2:9

BRIDE *Why are You standing behind the wall and gazing through the lattice?*

JESUS I cannot come into your house unless I am invited. I stand at the door and knock.[21] I search for you, just a glimpse of you. My church will so often not let Me in. How then can I be with My bride? I must call to her, call her out from that house, so that she can be with Me.[22] Come out My love and be with Me. If your house is keeping you from Me, come out. If walls of religion are separating us, then come out. I long for your company. I am searching for you, gazing through the lattice, longing for a glimpse of you. Oh, come out and be with Me. Don't let anything come between us and our love.

Song 2:10

JESUS   Rise up My love, My fair one, and come away with Me. Let us run across the fields and the hills together. Let us enjoy freedom together. The sun is shining, it is warm and beautiful. Do not stay indoors where it is dark and dismal. Come outside with Me into the light, and into the warmth of My embrace.

Song 2:11

BRIDE   *What do you mean – the winter is passed?*

JESUS   The winter is the dormant season. Nothing grows in winter. The winter is over. It is time for growth. It is time for harvest.[23] Come and join Me in the harvest. It is time to rejoice in what I am doing on the earth.

Song 2:12

JESUS   A time of great rejoicing is here. The voice of the turtledove is heard in the land. My Spirit is beginning to call out across the earth. As His voice is heard He will call men to Me.[24] They will hear His voice and come running to Me, for the time for harvest is here.

Song 2:13

JESUS   The whole earth is about to blossom in a way that has never been before. As My Spirit is poured out on all flesh,[25] as the voice of the turtledove is heard in the land, the fig tree will put forth her green figs and the vines the tender grapes. My Father has been working.[26] The seeds have been sown, the watering has been done and now it is time for harvest, so rise up My love, My fair one and come away with Me. There is work to be done. It is time to rejoice as the harvest comes home.

Song 2:14

BRIDE   *Lord, why am I Your dove?*

JESUS   The dove is gentle and soft and kind. The dove is a symbol of the Holy Spirit, and He now dwells in you. You have His character and you reflect Him. You are beautiful as He is beautiful. I want you to come away with Me to the secret place where no one can disturb us, where we can be together, and where we can share those intimate moments. I want to be with you, just to see your face and to hear your voice as you worship Me – as you embrace Me. As you worship Me your voice is sweet in My ear. As you lift your hands, as you lift your face to Me in adoration, you enrapture My heart, for your face is lovely, your whole countenance shines with your love for Me. You are radiant, My bride, and I adore you.

Song 2:15

BRIDE   *Can You explain verse 15. Who are the brothers talking to, and what are the little foxes?*

JESUS   The little foxes are those things that would spoil

your fruit. I am the vine and you are the branches and you will bear much fruit as you abide in Me.[27] However, there are little things that occur in your lives that would spoil that fruit. The enemy will send in the little foxes who will steal the fruit. The big foxes cannot get in, for you are guarding against those – the major temptations and major sins. No, it is the little things that creep in un-noticed that do the damage. A little bit of offence here, a little bit of jealousy there. It is the things that are not obvious – your attitudes, your feelings, your relationships. The fruit of the Spirit is love, joy, peace etc.[28] The enemy will attempt to steal your fruit by sending little things, little temptations, that will spoil that fruit.[29] Always be on your guard against the subtleties of his attack. Do not be offended with each other,[30] do not be bitter or jealous,[31] but give preference to one another in love.[32] Allow My love to flow through you, and out of you, to each other. Guard against the little things that spoil the fruit. Catch the little foxes before they come between us, for if you allow them in, they will not only spoil your relationships with one another, but they will spoil our love too. So guard against the little foxes, the thoughts and temptations, the feelings and attitudes that are not of Me.[33] The enemy will send them to you. Be on your guard all the time. Do not let him spoil our love – the fruit of the vine.

Song 2:16

JESUS   My bride, you are Mine. You are betrothed to Me.[34] I have paid the bride price for you. It was a great price,[35] but it was well worth it. You are Mine now and no one, no one, can separate us. No one can snatch you out of My arms. We are in covenant with each other, promised to each other. We have shared the cup of the covenant together and that is eternal.[36]

BRIDE   *What does feeding Your flock among the lilies mean?*

JESUS   You are the lily of the valley. You are the lily among thorns. You are beautiful to Me and I want you to help Me feed My sheep. As I said to Peter, 'Feed My sheep, feed My lambs'.[37] I have many little ones to bring in to My flock, and I want you to help Me feed them. Give them My word, teach them, nurture them, show them how to praise Me, how to worship Me, so that they too can have that intimate relationship with Me. Many of them will be distressed, hurt, frightened, disorientated as they come out of the world where they have been savaged by wolves. Bring them into My sheep pen where there is protection and safety and peace.[38] Feed them, nurture them and restore them. Show them My love for them and I will heal their hurts and make them whole again.

Song 2:17

BRIDE   *Lord, will You explain verse 17*

JESUS   The daybreak is coming. The morning star is rising.[39] The sun of righteousness is rising. I am the Sun of Righteousness,[40] the Morning Star, and I am coming soon. But until that day there is separation, in the sense that we cannot physically be together. When the day breaks and I return, the shadows will flee away, for the brightness of My coming[41] will destroy all darkness.[42] In that day, and it will be soon, we will be together. In that day will be My wedding[43] and we will be joined forever, both in the Spirit and in the natural – or super-natural. Until then there are shadows and we both have our roles to play, and we can only be together in the Spirit. But the daybreak is almost here. The darkest hour is just before dawn and the darkest hour is here now.[44] Wait and watch for the dawn, My love. It is coming.

Song
of
Solomon

CHAPTER THREE

Song 3:1-2

BRIDE   *Lord, why couldn't the Shulamite find You?*

JESUS   Go back to the previous verse. Remember, the chapters and verses were added later. Always go back to get the flow. We talked about the separation until the daybreak, until the time of My coming. There is a longing in the heart of My bride for the day we can be together physically. In that sense you cannot find Me yet. It's as though we correspond by letter, only it's much more than that, for My Spirit is fused to your spirit and I can talk to you directly.[1] But for now there is the physical separation.

BRIDE   *Lord, the flow of thoughts has stopped. Are You trying to show me something?*

JESUS   I am creating a hunger in you. I want you to appreciate what we are doing and that it is not you. When the flow stops it reinforces that it is Me speaking to you. When you cannot hear My voice then you will know an emptiness, a separation, that will cause you to seek Me again. My bride must long to be with Me beyond anything else. The Shulamite was desperate when she could not find Me, and she went searching. Are you, My bride, so desperate for My presence that you will go out into the night to search for Me?[2] Sometimes I withdraw slightly just to test you, to see what you will do. I will never leave You,[3] but I want to create a hunger in you for Me so that you will know the difference when I am not there, and you will seek Me diligently and find Me.[4] The Shulamite arose and went into the city to find Me. She did not care about her reputation[5] because she was so desperate to be with Me. Do you, My bride, care so much about Me, that you would care nothing for your reputation? Would you search for Me with such desperation if I was not there? I hope that you would, because I searched for you. When you were a lost sheep I searched desperately for you, I searched diligently for you, until I found you.[6] Will you search for Me like that? Do I mean as much to you as you do to Me? You have no idea how much I long to be with you. When I withdraw from you it is to test your heart. Not so that I would know your heart, I already know your heart,[7] but I test your heart so that you will know your heart, so that you will know how important I am to you, so that you will know if you will search for Me until you find Me.

Song 3:3

BRIDE   *Who are the watchmen who go about the city?*

JESUS The watchmen are those who are awake. Those who are awake see what is happening. They know where I am and what I am doing.[8] They are the ones who are guarding the flock. Satan will not catch them by surprise for they are listening to My voice. They are alert and tuned in. They hear My voice and they see – in the Spirit, and they hear – in the Spirit. They are My prophets for they hear what I say, and they see what I am doing,[9] and they tell the people. They respond in prayer and intercession to what they see and hear and they guard the flock in the night.

Song 3:4

BRIDE *Lord, talk to me about verse 4*

JESUS When you find Me will you cling to Me? Will you refuse to let Me go? Is our relationship so important to you that you will forsake everything else to be with Me,[10] to ensure there is no separation? Will you bring Me into the secret place of the chamber of your heart and keep Me there and not let Me go? Or will you allow the things of this world to creep in again and gradually push Me out?[11] No, once you have found true love you will not let anything come between us. Lock the door and do not let Me go again. Do everything necessary to keep this intimacy and let nothing come between us.

BRIDE *Why did the Shulamite bring you into her mother's chamber?*

JESUS The Shulamite's mother is the one who conceived her and brought her up. In spiritual terms, the one who conceived you and brought you up was the church.[12] When you have found Me, bring Me into the church. I have been standing at the door knocking.[13] Now that you have found Me, bring Me in and do not let Me go. I am not talking about the building, but the body of My people. Where two or three are gathered, there I am in the midst of them.[14] In that sense the church is your mother. Bring Me into your mother's chamber. When you meet together you are the church and form a chamber, a dwelling place.[15] If each of you brings Me in with you, I will be there in the midst of you. Let each new believer who finds Me bring Me back to that chamber. It is a safe place. As you, the church, pray for the unsaved they respond to Me. They are conceived in the church and so it is right that they should return with Me to the place where they were conceived.

Song 3:5

JESUS   Oh Daughters of Jerusalem, do you want a love such as this? Do you want Me with such a passion as this? Are you desperate enough yet for My love? If you are, then come to Me and I will satisfy your hunger and your thirst.[16] I am desperate for you, but I must wait until you long for Me with that same passion and longing. I do not want a half-hearted relationship. I want all or nothing. If you are lukewarm I will spew you out of My mouth.[17] You are to be My bride and I want total commitment to our love. Nothing less will satisfy Me. Nor will it satisfy you. Come to Me when you are ready, Oh daughters of Jerusalem. I am waiting and longing for you.

Song 3:6

BRIDE   *Lord, will You explain verse 6*

JESUS   Do you remember that after I was baptised by John, the Spirit drove Me into the wilderness for forty days and forty nights during which time I was tempted by the devil. I came out of that wilderness victorious and in the power and might of Jehovah.[18] The Holy Spirit was upon Me, empowering Me to begin My ministry. The pillars of smoke represent the Spirit. The pillar of fire and smoke went before the children of Israel in the wilderness.[19] That is My Spirit, and that same Spirit, that same anointing, and same empowering, is available for you, My bride, as you fulfil what I call you to do.[20] Remember I was given gifts of frankincense and myrrh by the wise men after My birth.[21] As I went to the cross I was a sweet smelling sacrifice[22] to My God and to your God.

Song 3:7

BRIDE   *What about Solomon's couch and the sixty valiant men?*

JESUS   This speaks of My kingly authority. I am coming again out of the wilderness, to take up My throne. I am seated in heavenly places on My throne,[23] but My throne is about to come to earth, borne by the armies of heaven.[24]

Song 3:8

JESUS   There is fear in the night. A dark night is coming

on the earth[25] and there is great fear coming on those who do not know My name, those who do not carry My name on their foreheads.[26] The darkest hour is just before dawn. When things are at their blackest, when the antichrist is reigning and My Father's judgements are being poured out on this wicked and unrepentant generation,[27] when things cannot possibly get any worse and there is deep darkness on the earth, then I will burst forth from the heavens with My sword on My thigh and the armies of heaven at My side.[28] Glorious light will flood the earth[29] and the darkness will flee away. Look for that day. It is coming soon.

Song 3:9

JESUS The wood of Lebanon represents My people. The cedars of Lebanon are My people growing tall and strong.[30] Out of them I have made My throne. Out of your praise and worship I have built Myself a throne, for I inhabit the praises of My people.[31]

Song 3:10

JESUS The silver, gold and purple all represent My kingly authority, but it is you, My bride, who have paved its interior with love, as you have worshipped Me and spent time with Me in sweet embrace. We will share this throne together as you rule and reign with Me.[32]

BRIDE *Why is this a portable chair?*

JESUS My kingdom is the whole earth. Although My throne and kingly seat is in Jerusalem,[33] I must rule the whole earth.[34] It speaks of My ability to move throughout the earth.

Song 3:11

BRIDE *Lord, will You explain verse eleven?*

JESUS The daughters of Zion, or daughters of Jerusalem, My bride, are longing to see Me come. Remember we are separated for now but when I come we shall be together. My bride cannot wait for that day.[35] She is longing for Me to come – peering into the distance to see if she can see Me. Behold, I am coming soon. That day is almost here. Wait for it. It will surely come.

BRIDE *What does it mean by the crown which Your mother gave You on the day of Your espousals?*

JESUS The day I was crowned was the day I defeated Satan. Up until that day he was the ruler of the earth.[36] But I took his authority from him and handed it back to My Father.[37] My Father then gave Me all authority in heaven and on earth[38] and I led Satan captive in triumphal procession.[39] I then sat down at the right hand of My Father[40] and He crowned Me as King of kings and Lord of lords.[41] On that day He declared to Me that I was His Son,[42] the first of those to be born from the dead.[43] That is the day I was engaged to My bride – My reward.[44] My bride is My very great reward for My obedience to My Father, even unto death on the cross.[45] My reward is not My crown, My authority, My possession of the earth and all that is in it, for they were Mine anyway.[46] I willingly gave them up for a season[47] so that I could have the one thing I did not already possess, and that thing is you My bride. I could not possess you, even though I created you. I could not possess you and I could not possess your love. I had to win you and win your love. You had to come to Me of your own free will and that is My very great reward – that you have indeed come to Me and given Me your love. My happiness and My joy is now complete – in you.

Song
of
Solomon

CHAPTER FOUR

Song 4:1

BRIDE *Lord, talk to me about verse 1*

JESUS You are fair My love. You are beautiful, My bride. You are so pure and lovely. I can't take My eyes off you.

BRIDE *What does the veil represent?*

JESUS The veil hides your glory. As My bride you reflect My glory.[1] But for now it is necessary for you to have a veil. When Moses came down from the mountain his face shone because he had spent time in My presence. They put a veil over his face to protect the people.[2] My bride, as you spend time in My presence, and as I live in you by My Spirit, you shine with the light of My glory. But for the world's sake you are veiled at this time. But I know what you really look like – and you are beautiful and glorious. When the right time comes your veil will be removed and you will shine forth and the world will see you as you really are,[3] pure and without spot or wrinkle.[4] You are that already but the veil of the flesh is hiding it for now.

BRIDE *Why is the bride's hair like a flock of goats?*

JESUS As a flock of goats comes down the mountain side they appear to tumble down in a cascade as they all come down in one body. Your hair falls down from your head as you pull out the pin that is holding it up. It cascades around your shoulders. This is a sign of your virginity and purity and that you are not yet married. You will let your hair down for Me alone for you are betrothed to Me.[5] I am the only one who sees you as you really are and you are beautiful, My love.

Song 4:2

BRIDE *Why are my teeth like a flock of sheep?*

JESUS Shorn sheep are white against the background of the hills. They stand out in the sunlight. They reflect the sun and so do you. You reflect My light and My glory.[1] It's just a way of saying that every part of you is beautiful in My eyes.

BRIDE *And what about the sheep being washed?*

JESUS The shorn sheep have been washed and there is no dirt on them. They are clean. You are washed clean by My word.[6]

BRIDE *And what about them bearing twins?*

JESUS These sheep are not barren – they reproduce. They are fruitful. My sheep are fruitful and clean. They have been shorn and produced wool. My sheep are profitable to Me. My sheep also reproduce themselves in abundance. You are My sheep and you will reproduce yourselves abundantly as the harvest comes in. They will see that I am the Good Shepherd and they will join My flock as you tell them about Me.[7]

Song 4:3

BRIDE   *Why are my lips like a strand of scarlet?*

JESUS   Your mouth is lovely as you whisper your worship to Me. As your mouth speaks right things, as your mouth speaks My word back to Me, I delight in you.[8] Your lips have been cleansed by My blood[9] and that is why they are a strand of scarlet. I delight in you when I hear you speak My word, My truth.[10] Your lips are beautiful to Me as you speak good things, things that build up and edify.[11] Your mouth is pure and holy, touched by the fire of My love.[12]

BRIDE   *What about my temples being a piece of pomegranate?*

JESUS   Your temples represent your mind which you have renewed according to My word.[13] Go and look up about the pomegranate.

BRIDE   *The pomegranate has scarlet flowers contrasting with deep green leaves, yellowy brown fruit with a hard rind and a juicy pulp full of seeds. Their shape was copied round the edge of the high priest's robe and carved on the pillars of Solomon's temple. OK Lord, I've looked up pomegranate.*

JESUS   The scarlet flowers again speak of My blood. The tree is upright, and you are upright and righteous in My sight. The fruit is used as an ornament on the high priest's robes,[14] and speaks of your priestly office as king and priest to My Father.[15] The fruit was used as an ornament on the pillars of Solomon's temple.[16] In the next verse your neck is described as a tower, which is like a pillar, and your temple is described as a piece of pomegranate. All this speaks of what I am doing in your life. You are My temple[17] ornamented by pomegranates, that is your mind is renewed. You have My mind[18] and you are being changed from one degree of glory to another.[19]

Song 4:4

BRIDE   *What about the tower of David?*

JESUS   The tower of David stood tall over the city – your neck is tall and graceful. Just as David hung shields on the tower so I hang ornaments on your neck. I want to adorn you with beautiful things. As you allow My Spirit to have His way in your life you are being adorned by beautiful ornaments.[20] As the tower of David was built for defence against attack so are you strengthened against the attack of the enemy.[21] The pomegranate has a hard shell and your mind is protected from the sharp arrows of the evil one.[22] As My Spirit controls your life[23] you are a strong tower which can withstand attack. I hang shields on your neck – that is the shield of faith.

Song 4:5

BRIDE   *What about my breasts?*

JESUS   Breasts speak of productivity – the production and nurturing of new life. They speak of the milk of the word.[24] They speak of suckling and comfort – of nurturing. You, My bride, are to suckle and look after those little ones, the little fawns, who have just been born into My kingdom. Look after them, comfort and protect them, feed them and supply their needs.[25] I am the one who is their supply,[26] but I mean that you should help them to receive from Me until they have grown enough to feed themselves.[27]

Song 4:6

BRIDE *Lord, talk to me about verse 6. Has this to do with the crucifixion?*

JESUS Yes it has. I've already talked about the dawn as the day of My coming. We are in the time of shadows now. This is the time of Satan.[28] There was a shadow cast over the land from the time of Adam, that is, the curse.[29] I had a specific mission to fulfil and that was the cross.[30] Look up myrrh and frankincense.

BRIDE *Lord, apparently myrrh is a pale yellow gum used as a spice and a medicine and in making the holy oil for the tabernacle and temple. It was also a pain killer which was offered to You on the cross and was also used to embalm Your body. Frankincense is a gum obtained by peeling back the bark of the frankincense tree. It gives a sweet scent when warmed or burned.*

JESUS Myrrh and frankincense speak of My death and sacrifice – a sweet smelling offering to My God.[31] I offered Myself for you. I stood in your place. I took on Me what should have been yours.[32] I did this because you are so precious to Me and I love you so much, My bride.[33] I love you so much that I would do anything for you, and I did do everything for you.[34] My love for you has not grown less but has grown more, day by day. If I did everything for you then, will I not do so even today.[35] You do not realise, My bride, how much I adore you. But one day you will fully understand My love for you – when the day of shadows has passed and the dawn is here – then all will be revealed in the brilliant light of My coming and you will know Me as I truly am.

Song 4:7

JESUS   My bride, you are beautiful, you are fair. There is no spot or wrinkle in you.[36] You are all fair. That is, each one of you is completely fair without spot. How is that, you ask, when we are still in the flesh? Remember the flesh is a veil that hides the true you. I see you as you really are behind the veil. I do not have to wait until you are perfect on the outside, for true beauty and true perfection is of the spirit behind the veil. You are not your flesh. You are not your mind (your soul) – you are spirit. You are a new creation clothed in My righteousness.[37] You are already perfect in My sight without spot or wrinkle. Do not be deceived by the outward appearance, for I see you as you truly are, and I love you just as you are. You are perfect in My sight. You are all fair. That is, each of you is completely fair and all of you collectively are fair. My bride is perfect, beautiful and lovely in My sight. I am enraptured by her and I cannot wait until we are together. But I must wait a little while longer, until all things are complete. When I come to take up My throne then we can be together and I will be complete in you as you are in Me.[38] We will truly be one as I have prayed the Father.[39] But see yourselves as I see you, My bride. Do not let the enemy deceive you. You are perfect, you are beautiful in My sight, without spot or wrinkle, for I see behind the veil of your flesh.

Song 4:8

JESUS Come away with Me, My love. Come out of the world system.[40] Spend your time with Me. I desire you to spend time with Me. I long for your presence. Let the world go its way, and spend time with Me. How can our love grow if you do not spend time with Me? How can we be intimate if you will not spend time with Me? Am I not more to you than what the world can offer? Come away with Me, My love. Come away with Me to the mountain tops. We can be alone on the mountain tops and we can see clearly from the mountain tops. The world is far below. You will see things in their true perspective[41] when you are on the mountain tops with Me, My love. Do not be enraptured by the world[42] but be enraptured with Me.

Song 4:9

JESUS For you have ravished My heart. I cannot bear to be without you, My bride. I love your presence. When you are away from Me I am empty and desolate. Even though all of creation is Mine, and all of heaven is Mine,[43] without you, My bride, it is as nothing. It is you I long for. I love you so much, My sister, My spouse.

BRIDE *Lord, how can the bride be Your sister as well as Your bride?*

JESUS You think in earthly terms. I am the firstborn from the dead,[44] the first of many brethren.[45] Therefore you are My sister as well as My bride. Do not think in terms of gender. This is a spiritual picture of My relationship with My church. Now, I was saying that you have ravished My heart with one look of your eyes. Your eyes are the windows of your soul[46]. As I look into your eyes I see to the very depths of you, into your true self, into your spirit and I love what I see. I see a fire and a passion blazing there for Me. I see a longing there for Me. I see that you love Me as I love you. You are fair My love. You are beautiful My love and I am ravished by your love for Me.

Song 4:10

JESUS How fair is your love, how pure is your love for Me. How much better than wine is your love for Me. How much better than all the spices is your love for Me, My fair one. I gave everything for you. I gave all that I had to win you, My love, for you are that pearl of great price.[47] You are so precious to Me, My bride. Come away with Me. Spend time with Me.

Song 4:11

JESUS Your lips, My spouse, drip as the honeycomb. Your words are sweet in My ear. As you praise Me, as you worship Me, it is as though milk and honey are under your tongue. As you kiss Me with the kisses of your mouth, in worship, you are a delight to Me. I smell the fragrance of My Spirit on your garments, the perfume of the oil with which I have anointed you.[48] I delight to smell that sweet smelling fragrance which I have given you as a gift – the perfumed oil of My Spirit. It is like an enclosed garden – heavy with scent.

Song 4:12

BRIDE *Lord, why am I a garden enclosed and a spring shut up and a fountain sealed?*

JESUS You are My garden. You are My special place. You belong to Me and Me alone.[49] You are locked and barred to the world. I want you for Myself. I don't want you flirting with the world. You are My virgin, My bride and belong to no one else. Therefore you are an enclosed garden set aside for Me alone. Your beauty, your fragrance, your delights are for Me. You belong only to Me and I will not share you with the world.[50] You are holy and pure and I delight in you. Open up to Me only. Let Me in to My garden that I may delight in you and have fellowship with you. Open your secret place of the heart and let Me in, so that we can be intimate together. That is what I long for and desire more than anything else – to come into My garden and enjoy it. You are a spring of living water that is shut up. I want to release you into all that I have for you. You are a fountain sealed. You have so much potential that I have built into you. Let Me into My garden so that I can release that spring and that fountain that I have placed within you. As that living water is released in you it will flow from you, out of the garden and into the world.[51] This is what I desire for you, that you fulfil the potential I have placed in you, that you be a blessing to a dry and thirsty world. As you let Me into My garden, into the secret place of your heart, I will uncap the spring and release the fountain so that rivers of living water can flow from you to, first of all, water My garden, but then to flow out of My garden to all those who are thirsty and dry.[52]

Song 4:13–15

JESUS   You are a beautiful garden, My love, My sister, My spouse, full of all that is beautiful, all that is true, all that is lovely and of good report.[53] There is nothing in My garden that is not fragrant and a delight to Me. I have planted what is in you, in My garden, and I delight in it. You are special, you are a paradise to Me and I love to spend time in My garden. You are a well of refreshing to Me, and to all those I bring to you, as they seek Me.

BRIDE   *What do You mean by 'all those I bring to You'?*

JESUS   You are My point of contact with the world.[54] As people seek Me I bring them to My garden where they can receive that living water from the fountain within you. As that water of My Spirit flows out of you, My garden, they will receive it and be made alive.[55] As you minister to those I bring to you, they will come to Me, for I dwell in My garden. I dwell in you by My Spirit, and as they come to you they will see Me, and come to Me, so that I can plant a garden in them too. The fragrance from My garden will be so beautiful, so delightful, that all will be drawn to you, and then they will be able to receive from Me, for I dwell in you. Indeed I am the fragrance that emanates from you.

Song 4:16

JESUS   Let the wind of My Spirit blow on you.[56] As you let My Spirit blow on you that fragrance will be released to the world. The Spirit will carry that sweet fragrance into the world where all is rotten and stinks. That sweet perfume will cause those in the world to take notice.[57] They will seek out the source of that fragrance. They will come first to you and then you can point them to Me.

BRIDE   *Jesus, come into Your garden and delight in me. Let me be a fruitful place for You. Cultivate Your garden and let me delight You.*

JESUS   You do already delight Me. You are a beautiful garden, and at the appointed time you will bear much fruit.[58] Let Me spend much time in My garden. Do not shut Me out, for I delight in you.

Song of Solomon

CHAPTER FIVE

Song 5:1

JESUS I have come to My garden and I have gathered much fruit already. You have produced much more than you think. You are a blessing to Me and I love you. But there is more, much more, for Me to do in My garden, much more time for Me to spend in My garden, and much more for My garden to produce. I am working on My garden all the time. Much of the time you do not notice what I am doing, a little bit here and a little bit there. I weed a bit. I plant a bit, and I water. Suddenly the fruit will come, at the appointed time. So do not be despondent if you do not think there is much fruit at the moment. There is an appointed time for fruit to come. I am the gardener. All you have to do is let Me into My garden and I will do the rest. My garden is a fruitful place and a delightful place. I am working all the time to make it so. Trust Me. I am the gardener and I know what is best for My garden and how to make it produce what I want.[1] Just let Me into My garden and I will do it. And as you bear much fruit you will satisfy those whom I bring to you. You will satisfy them with Me, as they drink from the fountain of My Spirit that I have placed in you, My garden.

Song 5:2

BRIDE   *I sleep but my heart is awake – explain that to me, Lord.*

JESUS   Behold, I stand at the door and knock. If anyone hears My voice and opens the door, I will come in to him and dine with him, and he with Me.[2] I am knocking at the door of your heart, My church, My bride. I want so much to come into the secret chamber of your heart, the intimate place. But so many of you are asleep.[3] You do not know that I am there. I am knocking and knocking. I have come through the night to be with you. I have come through the darkest hour of My crucifixion just so that I can be with you. But you are asleep! You do not hear Me knocking on the door of your heart. Wake up! Let Me in for the time is short. Oh My bride, wake up to what is going on, to what time it is in the scale of things. Behold I am coming soon![4] Wake up! Wake up! Do not be taken by surprise like the five foolish virgins.[5] Understand the times and the seasons before it is too late. My church sleeps while I stand outside and knock on the door. Open for Me, My sister, My love, My dove, My perfect one.

BRIDE   *I am awake my Lord, my beloved. Come into my heart,*

come into Your chamber and be with me. I long for Your
presence, to hear Your voice, to feel Your arms around me. I
am waiting for You to come and I am ready.

Song 5:3

JESUS   My church, My bride, has settled down for the
night. So many of you have gone to bed. You are not
awake, and you are not ready. You are not prepared to
make the effort to be ready for Me. I want you to be
dressed and ready for Me all the time. You do not
know at what hour I will come.[6] The bride does not go
to bed when she is expecting the bridegroom to come
for her. She is awake, dressed, and ready to go the
moment he comes. I am coming for My bride but so
many of you have gone to bed. Only those who are
ready to follow Me wherever I go[7] will be My bride.
Put your robe of righteousness, that I have given you,
back on.[8] Be unsullied by the world and by sin.[9] Be
ready for Me and watch for Me.

Song 5:4–5

JESUS   Behold, I am at the door. Do not leave it too late
or you will miss Me. If you are not ready and waiting
before I come, I will have gone by the time you open
the door. Are you yearning for Me, My bride? Are you
ready with your hand on the latch of the door? I am
coming for you. Be ready. Do not settle into com-
placency,[10] My bride, but yearn for Me, look for Me,
long for Me, as I long for you.

Song 5:6

JESUS Too late, too late! My church, My bride, was not
ready.[11] Oh, My heart is grieving for those who will
not be ready, for those who are too busy to be ready
for My wedding.[12] What else can I do to wake My
church up? I have sent My Spirit to prepare them, but
they would not listen, they would not accept what I
was saying and doing amongst them. Oh! if you have
ears then listen to what the Spirit is saying to the
churches.[13] Oh! I am grieving for My church that does
not want Me.[14] Oh! the sadness and the despair there
will be when they finally realise, and it is too late. But
you, My bride, My love, My fair one, are ready. My
bride is ready. You who have opened your heart to Me
and invited Me in are ready, for you and I have
intimacy together. We are not strangers and you know
what is on My heart.[15] You, My bride, are ready and
waiting, dressed in your righteousness, with the lamp
of your spirit filled with oil. You are not in the dark
that you should be taken by surprise, for you, My
love, are with Me all the time. We are one, and I am
coming for you soon.

Song 5:7

BRIDE *Why did the watchmen strike me and wound me? I
thought that earlier You said that the watchmen guarded
the flock?*

JESUS These are different watchmen. This speaks of the
persecutions that are coming. There will be a division
in My church[16] and a separation with the world.[17] My

church who are not ready for Me, who have not opened the door to Me, will turn against My bride.[18] They will follow the world system and New World Order and will hate My bride and persecute My bride.[19] This is inevitable for they hated and persecuted Me.[20]

BRIDE *What does taking my veil away mean?*

JESUS Your veil declares that you are betrothed to Me. They will attempt to turn you away from Me towards the antichrist.[21] But do not fear, they cannot snatch you out of My arms.[22] You are precious to Me and you belong to Me.[23] No one can take you from Me.

Song 5:8

JESUS My bride, I am putting in you such a passion for Me that you will be able to endure anything in order to ensure that you will be with Me forever. The troubles of this time will seem as nothing to the bliss there will be when I return[24] and we are finally together forever. Hold fast, My love, do not fear, for I am with you[25] and I will come for you. No weapon formed against you shall prosper[26] for we have the victory and I love you.

Song 5:9

BRIDE *My beloved is Jesus, the name above every name. My beloved is the Lord, the King of kings. My beloved is the One who shines like the sun. Why do the daughters ask about my beloved?*

JESUS   The daughters represent the church who have not
followed Me wherever I go. They do not understand
what is driving you. They do not have a love and a
passion for Me such as you do. They are satisfied with
religion and with old wine,[27] and therefore they
cannot see what is so special about Me that you would
run after Me. They are the five virgins who were not
ready and who missed the wedding.[28] I have a great
sadness for them for they have put other things before
Me, before My love for them, and I grieve for them. If
only they would have sought Me as you have done,
My bride, they would understand why I am above
every other lover. But they have been seduced by
other lusts, they have loved other things more than
Me, and they have made their choice.[29] If they would
turn to Me now, it would not be too late,[30] but the time
is coming when it will be too late. But you, My bride,
have sought Me and you are Mine. You understand
why I am more than any other beloved, for you have
tasted the new wine of My kingdom[31] and you will not
be satisfied with anything less.

Song 5:10–11

BRIDE   *Why are You white and ruddy and chief among
10,000?*

JESUS   When Paul saw Me on the road to Damascus he
described Me as shining brighter than the noonday
sun.[32] I am the Sun of Righteousness[33] and My face
shines like the sun in its strength.[34] I am the Light of
the World,[35] whiter than any white. I am the King of
Kings[36] and on My head is a crown of finest gold.[37] I

shine as burnished brass.[38] You have not seen Me yet as I truly am and you will be amazed, My bride, when you see My beauty and splendour.[39] And My beauty and splendour shall be yours also, My bride. When you are revealed to the world they too will be amazed as they gaze on you, for you shall shine as burnished brass, reflecting My brilliant light.[40] You are glorious, My bride.

BRIDE *Ruddy is a similar word to Adam which means red earth. Is there a connection?*

JESUS Yes, white means dazzling like the sun and speaks of Me as the Son of God. Ruddy is the same word as Adam and means to be rosy or red. This speaks of Me as the Son of man.

Song 5:12

BRIDE *Why are Your eyes like doves by rivers of waters washed with milk?*

JESUS The dove's eyes speak of the Holy Spirit.[41] He is gentle and kind and He is My Spirit whom I have given to you. You, My bride, are gentle and kind, for you also are filled with the same Spirit. The rivers of water again speak of the Spirit and how He pours Himself out into a dry and thirsty land bringing life wherever He goes.[42] You, My bride, are to bring life wherever you go in this world.[43] Being washed with milk speaks of washing by the word of God.[44] Wherever you go, you carry Me with you by My Spirit. Be gentle and kind, bring life-giving water to those in the desert where there is no knowledge of Me,[45] and bring them the milk of the word that they might be cleansed from their sin and come to a knowledge of Me. Let the world see Me when they look on you, so be filled with My Spirit and manifest My presence to those who are blind and do not see.

BRIDE   *What does it mean by fitly set?*

JESUS   You, My bride, are My eyes in this world. Your eyes are dove's eyes, the eyes of the Spirit, and you have been fitly set. That is, I have placed you in a right and proper setting for you. I have put you in the body in the right position for you to carry out the things I have for you to do. Your position in the body, and the place where you are, have been chosen specially for you as most appropriate for you, for that is where you will function at your best in My service.[46]

Song 5:13

BRIDE   *Why are Your cheeks like a bed of spices and banks of scented herbs?*

JESUS   I am a sweet smelling sacrifice,[47] a perfume and a fragrance that permeates the world. The world is rotten to its core and stinks. As I move through this world, through you My bride, I am a sweet smelling fragrance to My Father. You, My bride, are carriers of that fragrance wherever you go, for I am in you.[48]

BRIDE   *What about Your lips dripping with liquid myrrh?*

JESUS   Myrrh speaks of death.[49] As you speak My message to the world that sweet smelling fragrance does one of two things. It either brings life or it brings death to the hearer. How they respond to the message determines which it is.[50] You see, the word of God is a two edged sword. It cuts both ways, for it can bring life or it can bring death.[51] As you speak My word to the people they can respond in two ways. If they repent and turn back to My Father then the knowledge of Me is a sweet smelling fragrance to them and to My Father. But if they reject what you say then the words that you speak will bring death, and My presence, instead of being the fragrance of life, will become the fragrance of death[52] – that is of myrrh.

Song 5:14

BRIDE *Why are Your hands rods of gold set with beryl?*

JESUS This speaks of My kingly authority. I am to rule the world as with a rod of iron, meaning that My rule will be firm.[53] The golden sceptre is the symbol of My authority to do this, and My hands are as that sceptre. It is My hands that bear the nail prints, and it is as the Lamb that was slain that I receive My commission to rule from My Father.[54]

BRIDE *What about Your body being carved ivory inlaid with sapphires?*

JESUS You, My church, are My body.[55] It is you that is as carved ivory. Ivory is white and speaks of the purity and the righteousness I have given you. You are inlaid with sapphires for you reflect My glory as you rule and reign with Me.[56]

Song 5:15

BRIDE *Why are Your legs pillars of marble set on bases of fine gold?*

JESUS Do you remember the statue in Nebuchadnezzar's dream in Daniel chapter two?[57] That statue represented empires down the ages and those empires deteriorated in quality. They went from a head of gold, to toes and feet of iron and clay – not even a pure substance. Well, I am the final empire and I straddle the whole earth. I shall rule and reign forever. My kingdom will never cease and My kingdom is founded on pure gold. My kingdom is glorious and righteous and without end.[58]

BRIDE   *What about Your countenance being like Lebanon, excellent as the cedars?*

JESUS   Cedars speak of people.[59] I am the Son of man.[60] I am the firstborn from the dead,[61] the first of many brethren.[62] My people, My church, are an excellent people, perfect in every way[63] and I love them, for they reflect Me and My glory to the rest of the world.[64] Cedars are tall and upright. My church stands tall and righteous in the world, a symbol of all that I am, demonstrating to the world the ways of My Father.[65]

Song 5:16

BRIDE   *Lord, why is Your mouth most sweet?*

JESUS   My mouth is sweet for I always speak good things. I do not allow bitter water to mix with the sweet, as some of you do. You must clean up your mouths, My bride.[66] Only allow that which is good and pure and holy to come from your lips.[67] Only allow that which builds up and edifies to come from your mouth.[68] Stop the bitter water of gossip and ill speaking that pours out of your mouths.[69] Let your mouth speak good things only. Pure water and bitter water should not come from the same fountain. You are a fountain of My Spirit and He is gentle and pure and He seeks to build up and not to destroy.[70] Watch your words, My church, for they can be as a poisonous snake that seeks to kill, steal and destroy,[71] or they can be a fountain of life to those who hear them.[72] Watch what you speak, My bride, for life and death are in the power of the tongue.[73] Let your tongue drip with honey. Let it drip with sweetness, My bride.[74] I am altogether lovely, My bride. Reflect Me to the world. There is no darkness in Me for I am altogether lovely.[75] There is no shadow of turning in Me.[76] I am not double minded.[77] I am pure and holy and without blemish, without spot or wrinkle. Let that attitude which is in Me be in you also, My bride, for you are to reflect Me.[78] What do people see when they look on you? What do they hear when they hear you speak? Do they see and hear Me? Do you truly represent Me, My bride? As you submit to Me and to My Spirit,[79] and as you spend time in My presence,[80] then, yes, you will truly reflect My nature to the world, and, as they look on you, they will indeed see and hear Me.

BRIDE   *Yes, O daughters of Jerusalem, this is my beloved, my friend, my covenant partner, my bridegroom, and He is altogether lovely. There is none to compare with You, my Lord.*

Song
of
Solomon

CHAPTER SIX

Song 6:1

BRIDE *Where have You gone Lord, and why do the daughters want to find you too?*

JESUS I have withdrawn and gone to My garden. Will you seek after Me? Will you run after Me? I want to know how much you desire to be with Me. Will each one of you, My bride, seek after Me and find Me? Will you, My church seek after Me and find Me? If you will seek Me, you will find Me.[1] I am not far away. I am not difficult to find.[2] You, My bride, know where I am and you are to lead others to Me. There are many out there who are seeking Me but do not know where to find Me. They have tried here and they have tried there, but they have not found Me. You know where I am, My love. Will you lead them to Me? When they come to you saying 'Where is He?' will you lead them to Me. I need you to do this, for they are lost and there isn't much time left. I need you, My bride, to lead the others to Me so that My joy will be complete. Will you do this for Me, My love?

Song 6:2

JESUS I have gone to My garden, My love, for I have much to do there. My garden is My church and there is much to do to bring in the harvest. My church needs tending. It needs weeding. It needs looking after if I am to gather My spices and My lilies. My flock needs feeding and nurturing in My garden. The enemy has been at work in My garden, My church, and I need to put My garden in order before I return to gather from it what I have sown and planted. I am working in My garden, in My church, to restore it and put it in order ready for the day that I return to gather My harvest.[3] You will find Me at work in My garden, My love, for I have much to do in My church before I return to gather it to Me. You, My bride, are to bring the others to My garden so that they will find Me there.[4] So many are lost and looking in the wrong places and they cannot find Me. Go out, My bride, and find them and bring them back to Me where I am in My garden.[5] Do this for Me, My love, whilst I tend the garden for My Father.

Song 6:3

BRIDE *Lord, talk to me about this verse.*

JESUS My bride, I want you to understand the strength of the bond there is between us.[6] We are united by love, and My Father is love.[7] I am love. No one, and no thing, can separate us.[8] You belong to Me, My love, and I have paid a great price for you.[9] I have redeemed you from Satan's slave market.[10] I have bought you and you belong to Me. You are Mine. And I belong to you, for I have entered into a covenant with you.[11] I have promised to be your God and you can claim Me as your personal God on the basis of this covenant.[12] This covenant gives you, My bride, the right to ask of Me all that I have set out in My word.[13] As My bride, everything I have, everything I possess, everything that I am belongs to you. For you and I are one. You are so precious to Me that I would withhold nothing from you.[14] Because My Spirit dwells in you, and is joined to your spirit, I can trust you with all that I am and all that I have. In return you have offered yourself to Me. Although I bought you and paid a great price for you, I have not enslaved you. Instead I set you free to choose, and you have chosen Me from amongst all the other gods in this world. And I am so pleased, for I love you greatly. It is our love that binds us together. Yes, we are in an unbreakable covenant together that commits us to each other,[15] but it is our love that binds us together. You are Mine and I am yours forever.

BRIDE *Why do You feed Your flock among the lilies?*

JESUS I feed My flock in pleasant places and in rich pastures. The flowers of the field make a beautiful meadow, a pleasant place. I lead My people into pleasant places and offer them rich food – the food of My word.[16] My word is so rich that you will never exhaust it. As you keep feeding on My word I will open up more and more revelation to you.[17] Come into the pleasant place, the meadows where the lilies grow, and feed on My word, and I will satisfy you.[18] Yet always be hungry for My word for you will never be satisfied, for there is always more. I have so much to feed My flock if they are hungry for My word and for Me.

Song 6:4

BRIDE *Why am I as beautiful as Tirzah and lovely as Jerusalem?*

JESUS My child, you are a delight to Me. In all your ways you delight Me, My bride. You do not realise what joy you give to Me as I gaze upon you, for you are beautiful, My love.

BRIDE *Why am I awesome as an army with banners?*

JESUS You are an awesome army, My bride. I have set you against the evil one and he cannot withstand you.[19] You are wearing My armour. You come in My name with My authority.[20] As you work together in unity and in peace with each other you are undefeatable,[21] for I have already defeated the enemy. When he sees you coming, he sees Me coming and when he sees Me coming he flees,[22] for I have already defeated him and led him captive in triumphal procession.[23] Do not be afraid of him or his followers. You are awesome, My bride, as you march in My name. None can withstand you. So do not fear,[24] do not be timid, but be bold, be strong, for the Lord your God is with you.[25] Satan trembles when you approach. Realise who you are, My church. Realise who you are, and what power and authority you have in My name.

March forth and take the land I am giving you.[26] It is yours already. Go and take it. And as you do this I shall take delight in you, for you are Mine and you are a blessing to Me.

Song 6:5–7

BRIDE *Why should I turn my eyes from you, Lord?*

JESUS Your eyes have overcome Me. Your eyes are beautiful. They are the windows to your soul.[27] As I look deep into your eyes I see deep into you. I see who you really are, who I created you to be. I see the real you as I look into your spirit. Your spirit is the real you created in My image. As I look beyond the outward shell I am overcome by your glorious beauty, My bride. You do not know who you are, My bride, but you will one day, when your glory is revealed[28] – not only to the world but to you yourselves. You are so incredibly beautiful and perfect. You are the perfection, the height, the supreme act of creation.[29] There is no one to compare with you. You alone in all of creation are suitable as a bride for Me. Your beauty overwhelms Me as I gaze into your eyes, My love, for I see who you really are. One day the whole of creation, and the whole of heaven, will stand in awe of you, My bride, as you stand at My side clothed in the glory that once was Adam's.[30] I long for that day when you shall be revealed to the world, when I lift the veil from your face and your beauty, your glorious beauty, shall shine forth as you stand beside Me in My Father's kingdom, My lover and My bride.[31] You will indeed be lovely as Jerusalem, the New Jerusalem, that glorious city coming down from heaven to be My dwelling place on the earth forever.[32] I can't wait, My bride, I can't wait for that day. Turn your eyes from Me until it is time, for you overwhelm Me with your beauty, My love.

Song 6:8–9

JESUS   My bride, you have been specially chosen. Before the foundation of the world I chose you as My bride and you have responded to Me.[33] There are many out there who could have been chosen. Many were called, but you have been chosen because you said 'yes' to Me.[34] That is what makes you special. It is not that you are any better or worse than the others, but because you have said 'yes' to Me I can work on you with beauty treatments to make you perfect in My sight. Queen Esther spent many months being prepared for the king. Many virgins were called but she was chosen because she was willing to submit to the necessary treatment that would perfect her beauty.[35] You, My bride, have been chosen because you are willing to submit to the beauty treatment necessary to make you perfect in My sight. I have given you beauty for ashes, the oil of joy for mourning, the garment of praise for the spirit of heaviness that you might be called a tree of righteousness, the planting of the Lord, that I may be glorified in My bride.[36] It is your quiet, gentle and submissive spirit that endears Me to you.[37] I have put that new heart and that new spirit within you.[38] I have made you a new creation.[39] Because you said 'yes' to Me I have completely transformed you into a queen fit for the King. Because you said 'yes' to Me you have been chosen from all the other candidates who were called. You, My bride, are special, the only one, My favourite. You are the only one for Me and as I gaze on your beauty I am ravished by You. I long for the day I can remove the veil of the flesh from you so that your true beauty can shine forth and be seen by all those in heaven and on the earth.

BRIDE *Who is the bride's mother and who are the daughters, queens and concubines?*

JESUS The bride's mother is the church and the daughters are other brothers and sisters in the church – other believers. My bride is special because she has submitted to the beauty treatment necessary. Not all believers have been willing to do this. Many are content with salvation. Many are content with receiving the promises of the covenant. Many are willing only to go so far. They still flirt with the world.[40] They are not totally dedicated to Me. This causes Me great sadness – that five of the ten virgins were not ready. They had no oil. Many of My church are not ready. They are not full of oil.[41] They have not dedicated themselves to Me. My bride has to have a passion for Me above everything else.[42] She must be totally dedicated to Me and follow Me wherever I go.[43] She must be willing to lay down the things of this world in order to be with Me and to please Me. She must be willing to submit to all that is necessary to make her the perfect bride for Me. Many of My church, although saved, are not willing to do this. I am greatly saddened by this for they do not understand what they are missing out on. But you, My bride, have delighted My heart because you have put Me first in your life and you have a passion for Me that you have allowed Me to place in you. Keep your eyes fixed on Me, My bride, for I am the author and finisher of your faith.[44]

Song 6:10

JESUS   My bride, you look forth as the morning. I am the Bright Morning Star[45] and you are joined to Me. You reflect My glory and you will shine forth as the day, for I am the Sun of Righteousness.[46] I am the light of the world[47] and as the moon reflects the sun so shall you reflect Me. We shall shine together to be the light of the world in the age to come.[48] There will be no darkness then, for darkness will flee away. You are awesome, My bride, as you reflect My glory.

Song 6:11

BRIDE   *What does it mean for me to go down to the garden of nuts?*

JESUS   The garden of nuts is the fruitful place. The verdure of the valley is the green pastures that I lead My sheep to.[49] You are the fruit on the vine. I am the vine.[50] The pomegranates speak of your renewed mind. Are you being fruitful My bride? Are you producing what you should produce? Go down and check out what you are producing. Is the fruit of My Spirit evident in your life?[51] Check yourself out, My bride, and see. Is there love in your life, is there joy in

your life, is there peace in your life, is there patience
in your life, is there kindness in your life? Are there
signs that this fruit is developing? Go down to the
garden of nuts and check on the state of the vine and
see if it is budding. I have called you to produce much
fruit,[52] but first you must check out the fruit of your
own life, for only when the fruit of the Spirit is
evident in your own life can you go on to produce
other fruit. So, be wise and go down to the valley, to
the green pastures where the fruit trees grow and see
if they are budded. See if you are becoming more like
Me. See if your mind is being renewed[53] and if you do
have the mind of the Anointed One.[54] The more time
you spend with Me beside the still waters and in the
green pastures the more you will produce this fruit.
Keep checking yourself to see if the vine has budded
and if the pomegranates have flowered, My bride, for
I am working in you to produce that fruit.[55]

Song 6:12

BRIDE   *Why has my soul made me as the chariots of my noble*
          people?

JESUS   Look up 'my noble people' (Or *Ammi-Nadib*)

BRIDE   Ammi-nadib *means 'my people (is) liberal, free,*
          generous and noble'.

JESUS   The fruit of the Spirit is indeed growing in your
          life, My love. Slowly, slowly, imperceptibly the fruit is
          growing. You do not realise that the fruit is growing,
          but I know that it is, for I am tending My garden and I
          am nurturing that fruit. I am changing you from one
          degree of glory to another.[56] You are not aware of the

changes that are slowly taking place in you, but I am working on you to make you more and more like Me so that you will be fit to be My bride. Yes, you are already perfect in My sight for I see the end from the beginning, but in the natural you still need to develop and change. And that is happening. Do not worry for I am doing it. I am working on your soul, and before you are even aware of it, you will be My noble people. You will be free to be generous, to give out freely as you have received freely.[57] This is why you need to check that the fruit is growing. Every now and again, go to the garden of nuts and you will see the difference since your last visit, for I am working on you, I am developing you, and causing you to grow and become fruitful, for I need you to become more like Me so that you can freely give of My Spirit to those who do not yet know Me. You are the chariots of My noble people. The chariots are carriers, trans-porters. You, My noble, generous people, are the carriers and transporters of the Anointing. You carry the anointing within you wherever you go and you will bring that anointing to the world.[58] As you have received so you will also freely give. This is the fruit that I want you to bear, so that My Father will be glorified in these last days.[59] The glory of the Lord will cover the whole earth, but you, My bride, will be the chariots that carry that glory throughout the world before I return to establish My throne and My kingdom, and then the knowledge of the Lord will indeed cover the earth as the waters cover the sea.[60]

Song 6:13

BRIDE   *Who are Your friends, Lord, and why are You calling for me to return and where am I returning from?*

JESUS   My friends are the angels, your servants.[61] They delight to look on you also. They also are amazed by your beauty, for you are a higher creation than they. For you are created in My image and reflect My glory. Oh, My bride, return to Me. So many in My church are distant from Me and have gone their own way.[62] They are far from Me in heart. Yes, they go through the motions, they say the right things, and do the right things, but their hearts are far from Me.[63] There is no intimacy between us. They do not spend time with Me, they do not talk with Me, and their attention is focused on many other things. I want My bride to return to Me, to come back into relationship with Me. Some of My church are going to miss what I am doing because they will not spend time with Me. I will only share what I am doing with those who are My friends,[64] My covenant friends, and those are My bride. Many will miss what is coming because they are not spending the time with Me now. They are not being wise. Instead they are foolish. Return, My bride, return to your first love, or I will remove your lamp stand from its place.[65] Return, My church, return to Me and have relationship with Me. Spend time with Me and let Me delight in you. Let Me gaze upon you. Let Me love you as My intimate bride. Return to Me, My bride, oh return to Me before it is too late! Behold I am coming soon.[66] I stand at the door and knock. Please will you allow Me to come into your hearts.[67] Please will you have relationship with Me. I adore you, I love you so much. I want to be with you so much. It grieves Me, it breaks My heart when you shut Me out. Please, oh please, return to Me, My bride! Come away with Me and spend time with Me, My bride. Oh, I love you so much. Please return to Me and let Me spend time with you. This is the cry of My heart in these days, that My church would return to its first love. Without that intimate relationship there is nothing. This is what it is all about. Without this relationship there is nothing, nothing, nothing! Return to Me and let Me look upon you, My bride. Oh, return to Me, return to Me, My church, My fair one, My beautiful one. Do not prostitute yourselves to the world, but return to Me. Return to Me and give yourselves totally to Me, for this is what I desire from you more than anything else. There is nothing else that you can give Me that I really want. I want for you to give yourselves to Me, to spend time with Me. Oh there is so much I have for you if only you would spend time with Me and give yourselves to Me. Oh, I just want to love you. Return to Me. Open the door again and let Me into your lives again, My church, My bride, My fair one, and I will come to you and sup with you and spend My time with you in sweet intimate fellowship. You do not understand, My bride, you do not understand yet, My bride, how much I love you and want to be with you – but you will one day, you will.

BRIDE *Oh Lord, how can I love You like this? I do not want to grieve Your heart. I will return to You if You will help me.*

JESUS   Yes, I will help you. All I want, all I need is for you to say 'yes'. All I need is for you to be willing and I will do the rest. You do not need to strive for this, My bride. You do not need to strive to spend time with Me and to love Me. All you have to do is say 'yes', to be willing and I will put in you the desire and the ability to love Me. I do not want our relationship to be a burden to you. Instead, I want it to be a delight to you. Just be willing and I will work within you to cause this to happen. I am already doing this, am I not?

BRIDE   *Yes, You are, Lord and it is wonderful indeed.*

JESUS   Why? Why will My church not spend time with Me? Why do they reject Me and turn Me away?

BRIDE   *We are too busy Lord, we are too busy doing things, too busy with the world, too busy with church, just too busy, Lord. You are right – we just do not understand how much You love us and want to be with us. Open our eyes, Lord. Give us the revelation of Your love for us, Lord. Let us see how much we need You. Give us some understanding of Your love for us, Lord. Otherwise, how can we love You as You love us?*

JESUS   I am doing this. I am doing this, My bride. I am stirring up love in My bride and she is responding. Yes, she is responding to Me – all will be well, yes, all will be well, My love.

BRIDE   *Lord, what is meant by the dance of the double camp? What would You see in us, Lord?*

JESUS   I would see My bride on fire with a passion for Me. I would see My bride burning with desire for My presence. I would see My bride so consumed by Me that she has no thought for anything else. I would see

My bride with the same heart and the same mind as I have, a heart that hungers and thirsts after righteousness,[68] a heart that reaches out to the lost.[69] My heart, My bride, is to destroy the works of the evil one,[70] to tear down the strongholds he has built up,[71] to set the captives free and release those who have been bound by him.[72] My desire is to see the oppressed set free, so that they are free to enter into My kingdom. What I want to see in you, My bride, is the same heart and the same desire. I want you to go after those lost sheep and bring them into My fold. What I desire is for you and I to have the same heart and mind on this, My bride.

BRIDE *Lord, we want to have the same heart as You but You will have to do it in us for we can do nothing of our own.*

JESUS You are right, My bride, without Me you can do nothing,[73] and you are nothing. But all I need from you is a willing heart. If you will say yes to Me then I will do the rest. I just need your permission and then I will work in you both to will and to do for My good pleasure[74] and I will perform that which is appointed for you.[75] This is what I would see in My bride – a willing heart, a pliable heart, that will bend to My will. I do not desire performance from you, but a soft and pliable heart that I can mould into My image and work with, and then together we can do what has to be done.[76] If you will be like this then I can work in you and through you. This is what I would see in you, My bride.

BRIDE *Lord, explain about the dance of the double camp, or Mahanaim. Jacob called the place double camp or Mahanaim in Gen 32:2 when he met with a group of angels, that is, a camp of angels and of humans.*

JESUS The Shulamite was asking the beloved if he wanted her to perform a dance for him. I do not want a performance from you, My bride. I do not want you to perform, before Me, before angels, or before men. I want you to be yourself, to be sincere and submitted to Me. I want nothing from you other than this, that you love Me and are willing to submit to Me so that I can mould you into My image and change your glory from one degree to another.[77] Relationship is what I desire from you, not performance.

Song of Solomon

CHAPTER SEVEN

Song 7:1

BRIDE *Why are my feet beautiful in sandals?*

JESUS Your feet are beautiful to Me, My love, for they are shod with the good news about Me. They are beautiful because they carry you wherever you go, and where you go, you take the good news about Me. I dwell in you by My Spirit and where you go I will go. 'How beautiful are the feet of those who preach the gospel of peace, who bring glad tidings of good things'.[1] My bride, let your feet carry you wherever My Spirit leads you, and wherever you go take the glad tidings about Me. There are many who have not heard yet, who do not understand yet. You are carriers of My anointing. It abides in you,[2] and it is My anointing that breaks the yokes of bondage that oppress My people.[3] I need you to walk, My church, throughout the earth carrying with you, wherever you go, the news of the good things, the news of how I came to destroy the works of the evil one[4] and to set the captives free.[5] Go, My church and proclaim peace and salvation to those who are weary, downtrodden and oppressed.[6] You are a Prince's daughter, My bride. Go and tell them that your God reigns,[7] and tell them that your Prince, the King of kings, is coming. If you will do this for Me then your feet will be beautiful indeed.

BRIDE *Lord, why are the curves of my thighs like jewels? What do thighs represent?*

JESUS Have you noticed that I am describing you, starting at the feet and working upwards? I am describing every part of you for you are fearfully and wonderfully made.[8] You are a glorious creation, My bride. I know, for I made you and you are Mine. You are the work of a skilled workman indeed, and I am that workman. You are a jewel in the crown of My creation. You are perfect and beautiful in every part. You are a delight to Me. Your thighs represent your ability to run throughout My world enabling your feet to carry the good news of My coming to all who will hear.

Song 7:2

BRIDE *Why is my navel a rounded goblet which lacks no blended beverage (mixed or spiced drink)?*

JESUS Your navel speaks of your belly, and out of your belly, or innermost parts, shall flow rivers of living water that will bring life to the dry and thirsty land of this world.[9]

BRIDE *Why is the drink mixed or spiced?*

JESUS Out of My side flowed a mixture of blood and water.[10] It is both by blood and by water that people shall be saved. Out of you will flow the living water and the testimony of My blood shed for the forgiveness of sin.[11] Your feet and your thighs will carry this testimony throughout the earth.

BRIDE *What does my waist represent?*

JESUS Your waist is a heap of wheat. Wheat speaks of bread. My word is bread to the hungry. You will bring My word to the world and feed them.[12]

Song 7:3

JESUS Again, your breasts speak of your ability to re-produce, to nurture and to feed. Your breasts speak of your productivity. As you carry the good news of Me, and provide water and food for My people, you will bring more and more little ones into the kingdom.

Song 7:4

JESUS Your neck is like an ivory tower holding your head up high. Hold your head high, My bride. Do not bow down to anyone but Me. You can stand tall in this world for you are Mine and I am yours. Let no-one put you down for I have created you, and set you apart, to rule and reign with Me when I return.[13] So hold your head high My bride, for you belong to Me. Your eyes are like the pools in Heshbon and as I look into your eyes I see Myself reflected there. Your eyes are clear and beautiful for there is no darkness in them, My love.[14] My compassion, My light shines out from your eyes, My love, and as the world looks deep into your eyes they will see only Me reflected there. There is a clarity shining out from your eyes that comes from the purity that is within you. For you are not a whitewashed tomb.[15] You are pure through and through, for I have made you so, and your eyes are like clear pools of crystal water that hide nothing for there is no darkness in you, My love, only beauty of soul, and clarity of soul. Perfection shines forth out of you, My bride. You have beautiful eyes indeed.

BRIDE   *What does my nose speak of, Lord?*

JESUS   Your nose speaks of your ability to discern the spirits. The spirits are as wind and the scent is carried on the wind. You can detect whether a smell is pleasant or not, whether it is pure or rotten. You can discern the spirits, My love.[16]

Song 7:5

JESUS   Your head is the crown of your being. Your mind is My mind, for I have placed My thoughts in your mind.[17] Your hair is like purple, and purple speaks of royalty. You are a royal priesthood, My bride.[18] You are to rule and reign with Me. You are the Prince's daughter, My bride, and you will stand at My side as I come in My glory.[19] The world does not know you now, but they will, and they will recognise who you truly are when you are revealed to them as I return.[20] I am captivated by you, My love. Even though I made you I cannot get over how beautiful you are and how wonderful you are. You are indescribable, My love, indescribably beautiful. Words cannot express how lovely you are. Oh, the beauty, the glory and the majesty of My bride is beyond description. The psalmist asked 'What is man that You are mindful of him?'[21] You, My bride, are the seal of perfection, full of wisdom and perfect in beauty,[22] and I have crowned you with glory and honour.[23] I have made you worthy to stand beside Me in the presence of My Father.[24]

BRIDE *Thank you Jesus, thank you. We recognise that without You we are nothing. Without You we would still be in the pit,[25] cast down lower than the fallen angels. But You, Lord, have raised us up and seated us with You in heavenly places and we love You. We will follow You wherever You go for You alone are worthy to receive honour and glory and power.[26] We worship You Lord and cast our crowns before You.[27] All we desire is to be in Your presence. Nothing else matters but You Jesus. We thank You Lord, and we love You and we worship You, our Bridegroom.*

Song 7:6

JESUS Your delights, My bride, that is, what delights Me, is your response to Me. You are soft and pliable in My arms. You are no longer stiff, rigid and un-yielding, but you are soft and you are pliable. We flow together as two dancers. We become as one and you respond instantly to Me as I guide you round the floor. That is a delight to Me, when you flow with Me in that way, for then I can give you the desires of your heart.[28] Continue to submit yourself to My leading, My love. Do not try to go your own way for then we will clash. No, submit to Me, yield to Me. Be a delight to Me so that I can easily guide you in the way that you should go, for you will be one with Me.

Song 7:7

BRIDE   *Why is my stature like a palm tree?*

JESUS   You stand tall and strong, My bride, and you are fruitful. Look up about the palm tree.

BRIDE   *It means to stand erect. It was the branches of the palm that were laid at Your feet at the triumphal entry to Jerusalem.[29] We will lay ourselves at Your feet, Lord.*

JESUS   No, My bride, you will stand tall and erect and wave your branches for Me as I return to take up My throne.

Song 7:8

JESUS   And I will come to My palm tree and take hold of its branches. I will gather you to Myself, My bride, as I come again. Never again will we be separated, My love, for you are Mine.

BRIDE   *Why are my breasts like clusters of the vine?*

JESUS   Fruitfulness My love, you are fruitful. You are the fruit of the vine. I am the vine and you are My fruit and together we make the new wine of the kingdom.

BRIDE   *Why is the fragrance of my breath like apples?*

JESUS   I am the apple[30] and I am in you. Breath is the same as spirit. I dwell in you by My Spirit and therefore your breath, your spirit, smells of Me.

Song 7:9

BRIDE   *Why is the roof of my mouth like the best wine?*

JESUS   Your mouth has the fragrance of the new wine. As you have drunk deeply of Me, My fragrance lingers in your mouth. You and I are one. I am in you and you in Me. You reflect Me in all of your being. Every part of you speaks of Me to those around you. They see Me when they look on you, My bride.

BRIDE   *Lord, what does the rest of verse 9 mean – the wine goes down smoothly for You moving gently the lips of sleepers?*

JESUS   The wine is our love and it goes down smoothly. That is, it is a delight to Me. Our love is a delight to Me. I am so overwhelmed by your beauty and your love that it is like wine to Me, like strong wine that intoxicates Me and lulls Me to sleep. You do not know how much I love you, and you do not know how much it means to Me to have you respond to Me, My love. There were no guarantees that any of you would respond when I went to the cross. But I would have died for you anyway because I love you.[31] But there was no guarantee that you would respond and love Me in return. But you have responded, and you do love Me, and that is such a blessing to Me. You do not know what a delight you are to Me as you respond to Me with your love. It is like intoxicating wine. It is My dream come true.[32]

Song 7:10

BRIDE   *Yes, Lord, I belong to You. I love You more than anything or anyone and there is nowhere I would rather be than in Your presence. You are a delight to me too, and Your desire is towards me.*

JESUS   Yes, My desire is towards you, My bride. From before the beginning of the world My desire was towards you. My Father and I created this world because Our desire was towards you.[33] My Father wanted children, born of His Spirit,[34] and I wanted a bride. Our desire was for relationship with a being who was created in Our image. You alone are created in Our image and are able to relate to Us on Our level.[35] This does not mean of course that you are Our equal, but that you think, feel and have emotions as We do. You sometimes wonder if We have emotions like you. No, it's the other way round. We created you to be like Us,[36] so that We could fellowship with you. You are in Our image, not We in yours. Our heart was toward you before the foundation of the world. Our very purpose in creating the world was so that We could have relationship with you. And now it is happening just as We planned. My Father has children, many children, who love Him, and I have a bride who adores Me, and worships Me, and who longs to be with Me. Soon it will all be completed and we shall be together for ever. We shall be in perfect harmony together. You and I, the Father, the Spirit, this world, and heaven, will be joined and become interlinked, and interwoven, as one creation. The natural and the spiritual will come together as one, and We shall make Our dwelling on the earth with you, and you shall dwell in heaven with us.[37] That day is coming. It will not be long now, and then we shall be together forever. Never doubt that My heart is towards you, for you are the apple of My eye, My own special bride, and you mean more to Me than anything else, for I died for you, and I rose again for you, so that we could be together.

Song 7:11–12

BRIDE *Why is the Shulamite calling You to go to the field and stay in the villages?*

JESUS The world is My field and I have sown My harvest. It is time for Me to go to My field to see if the harvest is ready yet, to see if it is time to gather it in. I came to My field before, but it was not ready for harvest, but now it is almost time and I will come back to gather in My harvest. Yes, the vine has budded, the grape blossoms are open and the pomegranates are in bloom. Indeed it is almost time for the harvest. Come, My bride, let us walk the field together and I will show you what to gather in. There is much fruit out there that is now ready to be gathered. Walk with Me, talk with Me, listen to My Spirit and I will direct you in where to gather and in what to gather. It is all ready now, ripe and ready for harvest.[38] There are so many yet to come into My kingdom. Won't you help Me, My love, to bring them in, to gather the harvest and bring it home?

Song 7:13

BRIDE *What is this pleasant fruit that I have laid up for You?*

JESUS The fruit that you have laid up for Me is that which My Spirit has produced in you, and through you. I am the vine and you are the branches, and as you have abided in Me you have produced much fruit.[39] That fruit is both in you and out in the world. You, yourselves, have grown, blossomed and matured. You have changed daily to become more like Me, and that is fruit – the fruit of the Spirit – love, joy, peace, patience, kindness, goodness, gentleness, faithfulness and self control.[40] This fruit abides in you and is produced in you, and My Father is glorified in this. But you have also produced much fruit in the world, as you have spoken to people, helped people, prayed for people, as you have been My hands, My feet, and My mouth in this world.[41] As you have ministered My love and demonstrated to the world who I am, you have produced much fruit and that fruit is now almost ready, and I want you now to help Me gather it in before the end comes and the harvest of the earth is reaped.[42] This fruit will be a joy and a blessing to Me and will glorify the Father. This fruit that you have laid up for Me is pleasant fruit indeed, My love.

Song
of
Solomon

CHAPTER EIGHT

Song 8:1

BRIDE *Why would I want You to be like my brother?*

JESUS It would have been out of order for the Shulamite to kiss her lover in public, but it would have been all right for her to give her brother a kiss. My bride, the times are coming when it will not be in order for you to kiss Me in public. The world system does not like to see the reality of our love and persecution is on the rise. Beware, My bride, even in the West, even in the so-called Christian countries of Europe, there will be persecution of My bride. Especially in Europe will there be persecution for those who love Me, as the new world order rises to power[1] and the spirit of Antichrist comes into the world.[2] So be forewarned, My bride, difficult times are ahead. They persecuted Me and they will persecute you,[3] because you love Me. But be bold, be strong, for I am with you.[4] Do not backslide, do not allow your love to grow cold.

Remain in Me, remain in My word, be obedient to My word and do not hesitate to obey Me. As you do this you will keep yourselves from being deceived. Many of My people will be deceived for they do not obey My word and their love grows cold.[5] But you, My bride, are different. You have responded to Me and there is a fire and a passion in you that will not be quenched. So, My bride, there are times coming when it will not be acceptable to the world system for you to have Me as a lover, and if you openly demonstrate that love you will be despised and persecuted of men. But you will not be despised and rejected by Me, for I love you with such a passion. Always remember that I am with you and sharing in this with you.[6] Indeed I have gone before you and shown the way. Yes, My bride, the days are coming when it would be more acceptable to the world if I was your brother. They will accept the worship of the world – that is the worship of false religions- but they will not accept that you worship Me. So if you worship Me publicly, that is if you kiss Me outside, then expect persecution. But this is what I want you to do, My love. Do not hide your love for Me. If you acknowledge Me before men I will acknowledge you before My Father when I come into My kingdom.[7] Stand firm now, My bride, stand tall now, and declare that you are Mine and you will one day soon stand tall at My side as we rule and reign together. We have the victory, it is already done.[8] Do not fear for I will support you and I will strengthen you for it is not by might, nor by power, but by My Spirit that you will overcome.[9] Delight in Me openly, My bride, and I will come in and sup with you, and we shall share intimate moments together. Remember that I love you. Remember that I died for you. Remember that I want to be with you for ever, and I want so much for you to be by My side when I come into My kingdom.

Song 8:2

BRIDE   *Why would I lead You into the house of my mother?*

JESUS   As I said to you before, the house of your mother is the church. Your mother is the church in the sense that the church brought you up. As you were born again[10] you were born into the church. The church nurtured you and instructed you and brought you up. It is right then that you should bring Me into My church. So many who say they are Mine do not acknowledge Me and do not want Me in the church. This causes Me great sadness. But I rejoice in you, My bride, for you do want Me, you do desire My presence, and you have invited Me into the house of your mother.

BRIDE   *Yes, Lord, I invite You into Your church, and I invite You into my life, for I am Your temple and You dwell in me.*[11]

JESUS   Yes you are right indeed. I do dwell in you by My Spirit and I am so glad that I do, for I can talk to you like this and share My thoughts and feelings with you.[12] This is how it was with Adam – I walked and talked with them and now I am able to do the same with you, by My Spirit being fused to your spirit. But the day is coming when we will walk and talk together in the flesh. I am looking forward to that day,

My bride. Are you?

BRIDE   *Yes, Lord, You know that I am. What does it mean by 'I would cause you to drink of spiced wine, of the juice of my pomegranate'?*

JESUS   Your love is better than wine to Me, My bride. Spiced wine speaks of My garden. Remember I am working in My garden to gather My spices. Your wine, that is your love for Me, is enhanced by My spices that I have grown in My garden. I have caused your love to grow and mature over the years. Now your love for Me is even greater than at first, and will become greater still.[13] This is as spiced wine to Me. The juice of the pomegranate speaks of the fruit that has grown in your life and that fruit is a blessing to Me. I eat of your fruit and I drink deeply of the wine of your love. Your love, your wine, intoxicates Me, My bride, and I cannot have enough of it. Keep bringing Me into the secret place of your heart, to the intimate place, where we are alone together, for this time is so precious to Me. Keep bringing Me into that place, My love, and cause Me to drink of the wine of your love forever.

Song 8:3–4

BRIDE   *Lord, why is Your left hand under my head and Your right hand embracing me?*

JESUS   You are lying in My arms, My love. You are in the place of intimacy. My left hand holds your head and My right hand embraces you. You are enfolded in My arms, My love. No one can touch you there. I am leaning over you, gazing down at you, looking deep into your eyes. You are so beautiful, My love, and I will protect you with everything that I have and am. You are so precious to Me, you have no idea how precious. I will not allow anyone or anything to snatch you out of My arms. My left hand cradles your head, protecting your mind and your thoughts from the attack of the evil one.[14] My right hand embraces you drawing you close to Me. Relax My child, My bride, for you are safe and protected.[15] Relax against Me and let Me love you, let Me caress you, let Me minister to you. You do not have to do anything but lie there and enjoy Me. Relax in My arms, rest in My arms, sleep in My arms, for I am with you and I will never leave you nor forsake you. As you lie there I gaze into your eyes in wonder and in awe of the beauty that I see there, deep in your spirit and your soul, and oh, how My heart races and throbs with joy as I see you smile back at Me. I see that love, that joy, that peace and contentment in your face as you rest in My presence. I rejoice to see that you are content in Me and that you desire no one else, and nothing else but to be with Me. You do not know how that makes Me feel, what a wonder it is that you have responded to Me. I gaze into your eyes and I see love for Me shining out of them. We are one, you and I, one flesh, one spirit, one soul, one mind. We are in complete unity and harmony. I prayed the Father that this would be so and it is so indeed.[16] Drink of My love, My bride, drink of My wine. We share the cup of the communion, the cup of the covenant, and we pledge ourselves to each other. We celebrate our love as we share in the new covenant. My body broken for you and the wine of My love poured out for you so that you would be Mine.[17] And now you are indeed Mine and I am yours forever. Rejoice My bride. Rejoice, My love, in this and let us celebrate our love together. Oh, I long for the day of our wedding when our love will be consummated.[18] I cry out to the Father for that day to come, but He says, 'In just a little while. Be patient, My Son, for that day will surely come. It will not be long now. It is nearly time. It is almost completed'.[19] And so, My bride, you and I must wait a little while longer. But keep looking for Me, keep searching for Me, keep saying 'Come', for I am surely coming. But in the meantime, My love, lie here in My arms in sweet embrace and anticipate the day of our wedding, the day when we will finally be together forever, and the day when our love will finally be consummated. It is coming – hold fast My love.[20] Do not waver[21] – stay in My arms so that I can love you and protect you and keep you safe for that day. Do not leave Me. Do not forsake Me, My love, and we will be together forever, one day soon.

BRIDE *Yes, Lord, I will lie in Your arms. Yes, Lord, I gaze into Your eyes with love and adoration. Yes, Lord, I desire no one and no thing but You and Your love. You have taken me out of the pit, out of the miry clay and set my feet upon the Rock.[22] You have given me new life, You have given me Your life, how could I love anyone but You. Yes, Lord, I will stay in Your arms and respond to Your caress for I love You more than anything. Oh daughters of Jerusalem, will you not love my Lord as I do? Will it not please you to lie in His arms? Do you not want His presence as I do? Daughters of Jerusalem, do you not know what you are missing? Let my*

Lord stir up love in you also. Let His love please you. Do not reject His love, but come to Him and share in His love with me.

JESUS   Yes, daughters of Jerusalem, My church, will you not come to Me, for I long to be with you also. I long for your presence and for your love. Oh, won't you let Me stir up love in you? Why do you want to remain outside My love? Why do you say you are Mine but won't let Me into your lives? Open the door to Me and let Me come in so that I can sup with you and be with you. I don't want to have to say to you 'I never knew you',[23] so turn to Me, and come to Me, whilst there is still time. Let Me awaken love in you too, oh daughters of Jerusalem.

Song 8:5

BRIDE   *Lord, why is the Shulamite coming from the wilderness leaning on You?*

JESUS   The wilderness is the world. Any place that is Godless, or without the knowledge of God, is a wilderness and a desert.[24] You, My bride, were in the wilderness of this world and you did not know Me. But I am bringing you up out of the wilderness into the pleasant places, into the green pastures, and you are leaning on Me. Yes, My love, I want you to lean on Me, and rely on Me, in everything, and for everything. I am your support and your ever present help in time of trouble.[25] You can rely on Me for I am faithful, I am true and I am just.[26] I will never fail you. I am not as a broken reed that will pierce the hand when you lean on Me.[27] I am constant and unchanging, and I fail not.[28] Yes, My bride, you are coming up out of the wilderness into a glorious place, and you are coming arm in arm with Me, leaning on Me and trusting in Me for everything. My word is a rod in your hand.[29] Lean on My word for it is a sure staff.[30] I and My word are one.[31] Trust in My word. Lean on My word, for it will support you in times of need. Renew your minds, My bride. Get My word into your mind and re-programme your thinking so that you have My mind.[32] The word that is deposited in your mind cannot be taken from you. Now is the time to be putting it in, to be renewing your mind, to be filling your treasure chest with good things.[33] Put My word into your mind now, and you will be able to draw on it later when you need to. My word will be with you always, and I will be with you always, supporting you and leading you, a strong staff for you to lean on in times of trouble.

BRIDE   *Lord, who is the relative who awakened me under the apple tree?*

JESUS   The relative who awakened you is the Holy Spirit. He acted as a midwife and awakened in you a desire for Me. I am the apple tree, the tree of life.[34] When you were in the wilderness you had no knowledge of Me at all, but someone, somewhere, prayed for you and the Holy Spirit came and dropped a seed of faith into your spirit. Your spirit was awakened, and quickened enough for My word to grow there.[35] As you heard the message about Me, that seed of faith grew sufficiently for you to take a step of faith and ask Me to be your Lord.[36] When you did that, the Holy Spirit came and dwelt in you making your spirit alive to Me.[37] You were born and brought forth by the church into My kingdom to become My child and My bride. I want you to listen to Me and do the same for others. Pray for those I put on your heart so that the Holy Spirit will have permission to awaken them too, for I can do nothing without you. I need you to intercede before I can move in someone's life.[38] You have the authority here on this earth and I need authorisation from one of you before I can do anything.[39] That is why you must pray, even though I know what you need before you ask.[40] Pray then for those who are lost in the wilderness, so that My Spirit can awaken them also under the apple tree that is Me.

Song 8:6

BRIDE *What does it mean for me to set myself as a seal upon Your heart and Your arm?*

JESUS You belong to Me. I wear you on My heart and on My arm. I can never forget you. Even if a mother could forget her child, I will never forget you.[41] Our covenant is the seal that binds us together and My Spirit joined to your spirit is your guarantee of this. You belong to Me forever and you have the guarantee of the Spirit that what He has promised through Me will come to pass.[42] You have a certain hope and a future.[43]

BRIDE *Is love as strong as death, Lord?*

JESUS No, My bride, love is much stronger than death. Death is from the enemy, but I am love, and I have conquered death.[44] I have taken the keys of death and Hades[45] and they will eventually be done away with,[46] but love is eternal, for I am love and I am eternal.[47] And now you, My bride, are also eternal for you are one with Me.[48] That is why nothing can separate us. Only you can do that, for you can walk away from our relationship for I have given you free will.[49] But why would you want to do that, My love, having tasted the wine of our love? No, My bride, you will not do that. I know that you will not do that, for you have pledged yourself to Me and you are Mine. No! Love is much stronger than death, and you love Me, for My love abides in you. Death cannot claim you, for you are Mine forever.

BRIDE *No, Lord, we will never leave You nor forsake You. Where would we go, for You have the words of eternal life,[50] and we have tasted the wine of Your love, and Your love is much better than wine. No, the world has nothing with which to tempt us.[51] Lord, what about jealousy being as cruel or as hard as the grave?*

JESUS Oh yes, My bride, jealousy is as cruel as the grave. Guard against jealousy, My love, for it can destroy you. Unchecked jealousy will lead to the grave and the flames of eternal death. Guard against jealousy with everything that is within you.[52] Jealousy is one of those little foxes that will spoil the vine. It can creep in unnoticed, and if unchecked will lead to offence, and a root of bitterness that cannot be dug out.[53] That will lead to failure to obey My word, and from there the door to deception is opened, and then the slide towards the fires of hell begins.[54] Oh, My bride, guard against jealousy with all that is within you. Be alert, stay obedient to My word[55] and forgive, forgive, forgive those who wrong you, or you imagine have wronged you.[56] Do not give the evil one a foothold. Keep the door tightly shut to him, My bride. Listen to My Spirit for He will tell you immediately, if you will stay tuned to Him.

Song 8:7

BRIDE *Lord, talk to me about verse 7. What does the Shulamite mean by 'love cannot be quenched or drowned'?*

JESUS My bride, love is eternal, it is the very essence of My being. It cannot be quenched or drowned for I am eternal. If My love dwells in you, if I dwell in you by My Spirit, then love cannot fail. Faith, hope and love abide, for these three are My nature, but the greatest of these is love, for I am love.[57] My child, if My love abides in you then your love for Me, and your love for your brothers and sisters, cannot fail.[58] When the enemy comes against you like a flood,[59] then your love cannot be destroyed, it cannot be swept away and it cannot be put out. Let the fire of My love burn brightly in you, My bride. Let your love for Me, and your love for each other, burn brightly, for it is the flame of My love burning in you that will attract others to Me. How brightly is the flame of My love burning in you? A weak flame will be put out by water, but a strong flame will turn water to steam and evaporate it. How hot is the flame burning in you, My love? Will it evaporate the water the enemy throws at you, or will he be able to extinguish your love for Me? Burn brightly, My bride. Let Me build a furnace in you that nothing will extinguish. Let Me put a fire in your spirit that will burn eternally, as My love for you is eternal. How priceless is My love? How much do you desire My love? What will you give for My love? I gave everything to obtain your love. Will you do the same for Me? Will you give up everything to obtain My love?[60] My love is priceless. There is no price you could pay to buy My love.[61] That is why I give it freely to all who would ask.[62] But do not stir up love until it pleases for My love in you is an all consuming fire.[63] It will burn up anything which is not pure gold, or silver, that is in you.[64] My love is a purifying fire, hotter than any earthly flame, and it will destroy anything in you that is not pure and holy.[65] Do you want this purifying fire burning in you, My love? It is an all consuming fire – the fire of My love.

BRIDE   *Yes, Lord, burn brightly in me. Consume all that is not pure and holy and that will not stand the test of time. I want to be like You, Lord.*

JESUS   You shall be like Me. I have placed in you the fire of My love and the waters will never drown it nor extinguish it, for I am changing you from one degree of glory to another. I am refining you and purifying you until you are so pure and transparent that My glory and My love shall shine forth out of you without any hindrance. They will see Me when they look on you, My bride.

Song 8:8–9

BRIDE   *Lord, talk to me about verses 8 and 9*

JESUS   My bride, when you come to Me, come as little children.[66] Do not be sophisticated and all grown up. It is the innocence of the children that I like. They do not question or argue. They are not full of their own ideas and their own importance. They come running to Me because they love Me and because they trust Me. They have questions, yes, but they accept the answers that I give. My church considers itself too grown up and too sophisticated to do this. My church will not accept what I say, that is, My word. They want to argue about it, dissect it and pull it to pieces instead of just believing what I say. Oh that you would come to Me as little children, loving Me and trusting Me in everything. Children have perfect trust and I want you to be like that, My bride. Come to Me in innocence and purity and I will bless you.

BRIDE   *What are the brothers saying to the Shulamite?*

JESUS   The brothers are looking at the character of My bride. They are asking if she is pure and holy, or is she open to anyone or anything. The world looks at you, My bride, to examine your character. They are looking to see if this is real. The world plays around and are like an open door. They accept all that is put before them. They will try this religion and they will try that. They worship the occult and the new age, but they are not constant. They are as harlots open to every new idea. What about you, My bride? Are you as a wall? Are you enclosed by a wall of protection? Are you betrothed to Me alone? Are you a virgin?[67] This is what the world is looking for – to see if you are different, to see if you are for real. Are you for real, My bride? Are you chaste, My bride – not flirting with the world?[68] I want you to be innocent as a child, My love. I want you set apart for Me alone. If you are a wall, My love, closed to all but Me, then I will heap riches of silver upon you ready for our wedding day. You are spoken for, My love, you belong to Me alone. Do not be as an open door to the world, but be innocent, pure and holy. Let there be an enclosing wall around you that keeps you separate for Me. Shut yourselves off from the influences of the world. Guard your hearts and your minds.[69] Do not flirt with the world but keep yourselves innocent, pure and holy for Me, My bride, My love, My fair one.

Song 8:10

BRIDE *Why does the Shulamite say that her breasts are like towers?*

JESUS Yes, you are as a wall, My love. You are protected from the world's influence. You have built a wall around you to keep the world at bay, for you are Mine and you belong to Me. You are growing up, My love, in all innocence and purity, for I am keeping you that way. You are maturing, My love, and you are becoming very beautiful. You are no longer a child, but you are almost ready to be My bride. I love you so much and I long for that day.

BRIDE *What does she mean by becoming as one who has peace?*

JESUS As you grow up, My child, and as you mature you become as one who has peace. You have My peace, for that is what I left with you.[70] My peace passes all understanding,[71] for My peace comes from having a perfect trust in the Father in all circumstances and in all situations.[72] It is knowing that He has a perfect plan for you, that He is with you at all times and that He fails not.[73] I had peace when I went to the cross for in the midst of all that horror, which you cannot begin to comprehend or understand, I had perfect trust in My Father. Even though He had to abandon Me[74] I still knew that He would come for Me and lift Me back up to be with Him.[75] My, bride, you have that peace, the same peace that I had, because I have given it to you. Your peace comes from knowing that you are saved, that you are Mine, and that no one, and no thing, can ever separate us.[76] Nothing can separate you from My love or from the love of the Father.[77] This is your peace – knowing that the Father is utterly trustworthy for it is impossible for Him to lie.[78] It is knowing that We are with you at all times and in all circumstances and We will never leave you or forsake you.[79] So be as little children, My bride. Slip your hand into the hand of your Father and walk with Him and talk with Him. Run alongside Him skipping with joy,[80] for in Him you have perfect peace.[81] And as you mature and grow up, My bride, you will stand alongside Me, with My arm around you, protecting you and loving you forever. In this is your peace.

Song 8:11

BRIDE *What does the Shulamite mean by saying that Solomon had a vineyard at Baal Hamon?*

JESUS A vineyard speaks of wealth and riches.[82] I have a vineyard which is My church. I gave up all the wealth of heaven in order to secure My vineyard. I paid everything[83] to obtain that pearl of great price,[84] My vineyard, My church. However, My church is much more valuable to Me than all the wealth I left behind in heaven,[85] for My vineyard is made up of people. All the possessions and all the wealth in the world cannot be compared to the value of people – to the value of you, My church. You are so much more precious to Me than any possessions. Do you not understand this yet? How much I love you? I have given everything to obtain your love and your fellowship. I have gained so much more than I had before when there was just the Father, the Spirit and Myself. The angels cannot compare with you, My church, for they were not created in Our image. We cannot communicate with them, nor have fellowship with them, as We can with you. They are just servants.[86] Yes, they are glorious beings, but even so they are just servants. But you, My church, are so special. There is nothing like you in all of creation, for you are like Us.[87] This is why the enemy hates you so much for you are where he wanted to be.[88] You are seated in heavenly places with Me.[89] Yes, I have a vineyard in Baal Hamon. I am now the possessor of a multitude. Millions of you have come to Me and become Mine. I am now rich indeed, rich beyond compare.

BRIDE   *Why did You lease the vineyard to keepers?*

JESUS   I had to go away for a time. I came and I bought the vineyard but I could not stay in person to look after it as I had to go back to My Father until the appointed time for My wedding (and that time is almost here!). I therefore had to lease it into the hands of keepers.[90] Some of them did a good job, but others have not. I have been greatly distressed to see how some of My servants have treated My vineyard. My vineyard has suffered greatly at the hands of some of those who were appointed. But also many of My servants have done a wonderful job, and despite everything, My vineyard is now flourishing. It is almost time for the harvest. The fruit is ripening quickly, and multiplying and multiplying, and I will come soon to reap My harvest from My vineyard.

BRIDE *Why was everyone to bring for its fruit a thousand pieces of silver?*

JESUS The fruit from My vineyard is priceless. No one could pay enough to buy My fruit. Only I could pay the price for you, My church. No one else can. And now you are not for sale. My fruit belongs to Me and Me alone. You are Mine, My church. You are Mine, My bride. You belong to Me and I will not part with you for anything. You, My bride, are priceless beyond compare and I am delighted with the fruit from My vineyard.

Song 8:12

BRIDE *What does she mean by verse 12?*

JESUS She is saying that Solomon is her vineyard. Am I your vineyard, My bride? Do you look to Me to meet all your needs,[91] both physical and spiritual? Am I your source of supply,[92] or do you look elsewhere? Many of My church look elsewhere for their needs to be met. Many will turn to the world and they never think of asking Me,[93] and believing Me,[94] for what they need. But I am truly your source of supply. You have nothing that has not come from Me, for everything has been created by Me and for Me.[95] I am the author and finisher of your faith[96] and you have nothing apart from Me.[97] So turn to Me, My church, look to Me for all your needs. It is My greatest desire to meet those needs. I don't want you looking elsewhere when I am your vineyard. But you, My bride, know this, for this is how you see Me. You have your eyes fixed on Me. You, My bride, cannot take your eyes off Me for you love Me as I love you. You are enraptured with Me, as I am with you. Oh, if only all My church would see Me as you do, My bride. Yes, your vineyard is before you, My love. Look to Me and look for Me, for I am coming soon to be with you.

BRIDE   *Why does she say that You may have 1,000 and the keepers of the fruit 200?*

JESUS   She is talking about My vineyard which is you, My bride. Those workers who have looked after My vineyard whilst I have been away are worthy of their hire[98] and there is a reward waiting for them,[99] but I shall have My vineyard, for you are Mine and Mine alone.

Song 8:13

JESUS   My bride, let Me hear your voice. I am waiting to come to My vineyard. I am waiting to come for you, My bride. I am waiting and longing for the moment we can be together, and I am listening for your voice crying out to Me, 'Come'.[100] I cannot come until you call Me, for you have the authority on the earth.[101] My bride must be waiting for Me, and looking for Me, and longing for Me to come.[102] Are you waiting for

Me, My bride? Are you looking for Me, My bride? Are you standing in your house, staring out of the window, waiting for Me to come? Are you? Are You? I cannot hear your voice, My bride! I cannot hear you calling for Me! Is your lamp lit[103] and placed in the window of your house as a signal to Me that I may come? My Father is about to give Me permission to come for My bride. The moment I have been waiting and longing for, for so long, is almost here. He has prepared a wedding feast for Me,[104] but is My bride ready? Are you ready, My bride?[105] Are you calling out to Me, 'Come'? Are you as eager for our wedding as I am My love? I am longing for this day. I am yearning for this day when you will come away with Me. I want so much to come for you and sweep you up into My arms, to lift you up and swing you round and hold you close to Me. I am coming to sweep you off your feet and carry you home to be with Me forever.[106] Are you ready, My bride? Let Me hear your voice saying, 'Come'. The companions are listening for your voice too. The angels are waiting to hear you say, 'Come'.[107] The Spirit is waiting to hear you say, 'Come'. Will you say, 'Come', My bride? Will you not say, 'Come'? I long to hear your voice, My bride. I long to hear your voice say, 'Come'.

Song 8:14

BRIDE   *Yes, my Beloved, we say, 'Come. Come! Come! Come Lord Jesus'![108] The Spirit and the bride say, 'Come'.[109] Come quickly Lord. Come quickly! We are desperate for Yo* *come. We long for You to come. Yes, our lamps a*

the oil of Your Spirit, for You have filled us and set us ablaze
with love for You. We place them in the window for all to
see.[110] *We say, 'Come Lord Jesus'. Come. We have our*
wedding garments on.[111] *We are clothed in Your righteous-*
ness.[112] *We are ready. We are waiting. We are crying, 'Come'.*
The Spirit and the bride are crying, 'Come'. Won't You come,
my Beloved, won't You come? Do not delay. We long for You.
We are searching for You with our eyes. We are staring at the
heavens waiting for You to appear.[113] *Do not delay my*
Beloved, but come! Come! Come!

JESUS   I am coming! Behold, I am coming quickly. I shall
not delay a moment longer than necessary. I am
coming for you, My bride, My very great reward. I am
coming for you. I am like a gazelle, or a young stag,
bounding over the mountains to be with you, My love.
I can see you waiting. I can hear your voice. I am
longing to be with you. Hold fast, My bride, hold fast.
Do not waver. Do not falter, for I am coming for you.[114] I
am on My way. My Father has given Me permission
and I am coming. I am coming! That day is here at last.
Behold, I am coming. Tell the rest of My church who
are still asleep.[115] Tell them, tell them, for I want them to
be awake when I come. They have only moments in
which to get ready for I am on My way. Tell them to be
ready for Me. Tell them! Tell them I am coming quickly,
My bride, for they do not understand the times.[116] But
you do, My bride, you do understand[117] and you are
waiting for Me, longing for Me to come, and I do
indeed hear your voice and I am coming soon. I am
coming very soon indeed, My love, My bride, My fair
one. I am coming for you. I am coming for you!

NOTES

**Song chapter one –
pages 13–22**

1. 1 Cor 6:17.
2. *Proskuneo* is the most
   common word translated
   worship and one of its
   meanings is to kiss
   towards.
3. Jn 13:23–25.
4. The author believes that the
   work of Jesus was to
   redeem the lost and to
   provide children for the
   Father and that His reward
   for doing this was to be His
   bride, and that the joy that
   was set before Him was the
   prospect of an intimate
   relationship with us: Ps
   18:20, Isa 40:10, 49:4, 53:11,
   62:11, Rev 22:12, Heb 12:2,
   Jn 17:24.
5. Jn 16:23–24.
6. Jer 32:27.
7. Ps 84:11.
8. 1 Chron 16:34.
9. 1 Kings 19:12.
10. Rev 2:7.
11. Jn 16:14.
12. Jn 20:22.
13. Jn 19:30.
14. Gen 2:7.
15. After the fall Adam
    passed spiritual death to all
    mankind but Jesus brings
    life (1 Cor 15:22). The
    author believes that as we
    are now new creatures in
    Christ (2 Cor 5:17) we now
    have the ability to share in
    the bringing forth of
    spiritual children through
    prayer and preaching the
    gospel.
16. Jn 17:21.

17. Jer 8:22.
18. Song 2:1.
19. Ps 133.
20. Ex 30:22–33.
21. Ezek 47:9.
22. Gal 5:22–23.
23. Ps 103:3.
24. Isa 53:4–5.
25. Matt 5:8.
26. 2 Cor 2:14–15.
27. 2 Cor 1:22.
28. Matt 26:28.
29. Isa 61:3.
30. Matt 6:22–23.
31. 1 Cor 4:5, Matt 5:14–16.
32. Jn 15:20.
33. Ps 23:1–2, Jn 10:11.
34. Isa 30:15.
35. 1 Pet 2:2.
36. Matt 5:14–16.
37. 1 Pet 3:3–4.
38. Matt 28:18–20, Mk 16:15–18.
39. Isa 4:4, Mal 3:2–3.
40. 2 Cor 3:18.
41. Matt 3:16.

Song chapter two – pages 23–34

1. Isa 9:6.
2. Jn 15:4–7.
3. Jn 7:37–39.
4. Act 10:34.
5. Ex 19:5.
6. Gen 2:17. It is a commonly held belief that this tree was an apple tree. However, Jeremiah chapter 24 talks about two baskets of figs, one very good and one very bad, corresponding with good and evil. It is therefore possible that the tree of the knowledge of good and evil was a fig tree. It was with fig leaves that Adam and Eve covered themselves.
7. Ps 34:8.
8. Jam 1:17.
9. 1 Jn 1:5, Phil 4:8.
10. Eph 5:18.
11. Jn 2:1–11.
12. Ps 91:1–4.
13. Matt 5:6.
14. Jn 15:1.
15. Rom 8:35.
16. Eph 1:6.
17. 2 Cor 11:2.
18. Matt 10:37–38, Lk 14:26–33.
19. Lk 9:62.
20. Jn 10:3–4.
21. Rev 3:20.
22. Rev 18:4.
23. Jn 4:35.

24. Jn 6:44.

25. Act 2:17.

26. Jn 5:17.

27. Jn 15:5.

28. Gal 5:22–23.

29. Jn 10:10.

30. Matt 24:10.

31. Heb 12:15, 1 Pet 2:1, Jam 3:16.

32. Rom 12:9–13.

33. 2 Cor 10:5.

34. 2 Cor 11:2.

35. Matt 13:45–46.

36. 1 Cor 11:23–26.

37. Jn 21:15–17.

38. Jn 10:16.

39. Rev 22:16.

40. Mal 4:2.

41. Matt 24:30.

42. 2 Thes 2:8.

43. Rev 19:7.

44. Jn 9:4, Isa 60:2.

Song chapter three – pages 35–42

1. Heb 8:11.

2. Ps 63:1.

3. Heb 13:5.

4. Deut 4:29.

5. Phil 2:5–7.

6. Lk 15:1–7.

7. Deut 8:2, Jn 2:24–25.

8. 1 Thes 5:1–6.

9. Amos 3:7.

10. Lk 14:33.

11. Matt 13:7,22.

12. Gal 4:26 The Lamb's wife, the church, is the new Jerusalem (Rev 21:10).

13. Rev 3:20.

14. Matt 18:20.

15. Eph 2:22.

16. Isa 55:1–3.

17. Rev 3:15–16.

18. Lk 4:1–15.

19. Ex 13:21.

20. Act 1:8.

21. Matt 2:11.

22. Lev 3:5.

23. Heb 1:3.

24. Ps 2:6, Isa 9:6–7, Rev 19:11–16.

25. Isa 60:2, Jn 9:4.

26. Lk 21:26, Rev 7:3, 9:4.

27. Rev 8, 9 & 16.

28. Rev 19:11–21.

29. Matt 24:27, 29–30.

30. Isa 61:3.

31. Ps 22:3.

32. Rev 20:4, Dan 7:27.

33. Ps 2:6.

34. Isa 9:6–7, Dan 7:27.

35. 1 Thes 4:17.

36. Lk 4:5–7.

37. 1 Cor 15:24.

38. Matt 28:18.

39. Col 2:15.

40. Heb 12:2.
41. Rev 19:16.
42. Ps 2:6–9.
43. Rev 1:5.
44. See Chapter 1 note 3.
45. Phil 2:8.
46. Col 1:16.
47. Phil 2:5–7.

**Song chapter four –
pages 43–54**

1. Phil 3:20–21.
2. Ex 34:29–35.
3. Rom 8:19, 1 Jn 3:1–2.
4. Eph 5:27.
5. 2 Cor 11:2.
6. Eph 5:25–26.
7. Jn 10:14–16.
8. Matt 12:34, Ps 19:14.
9. Heb 9:22, 1 Jn 1:7.
10. Ps 17:3–4, Prov 8:6–9.
11. Rom 14:19.
12. Isa 6:4–7.
13. Rom 12:2.
14. Ex 39:22–24.
15. Rev 1:6.
16. 1 King 7:18.
17. 1 Cor 3:16–17.
18. 1 Cor 2:16.
19. 2 Cor 3:18.
20. 1 Pet 3:3–4.
21. Eph 3:16, Col 1:11.
22. Eph 6:16, 2 Cor 10:4–5.
23. Jam 4:7.
24. 1 Pet 2:2.
25. Jn 21:15–18.
26. Phil 4:19, Ps 23:1.
27. Heb 5:12.
28. Rev 12:12.
29. Gen 3:14–24.
30. Gal 3:13.
31. Lev 3:5.
32. Isa 53:4–6, 2 Cor 5:21.
33. Rom 5:8.
34. Jn 15:13.
35. Rom 8:32.
36. Eph 5:27.
37. 2 Cor 5:17.
38. Col 2:10.
39. Jn 17:21.
40. 1 Pet 2:9.
41. Isa 55:8–9.
42. 1 Jn 2:15.
43. Col 1:16.
44. Rev 1:5.
45. Rom 8:29.
46. Matt 6:22–23.
47. Matt 13:45–46.
48. 2 Cor 2:14–15.
49. 2 Cor 11:2.
50. Jam 4:4.
51. Jn 7:37–39.
52. Isa 55:1.
53. Phil 4:8.
54. 1 Jn 4:17.
55. Ezek 47:9.
56. Jn 3:8.

57. 2 Cor 2:14–16.
58. Jn 15:5,8.

Song chapter five – pages 55–66

1. Phil 2:13, 1 Thes 5:24, Ps 138:8.
2. Rev 3:20.
3. 1 Thes 5:6.
4. Rev 1:3, Jam 5:8.
5. Matt 25:1–13.
6. Matt 24:42.
7. Rev 14:4.
8. Rev 19:8.
9. 2 Cor 6:14–18.
10. 2 Pet 3:3–4.
11. Matt 25:11–12.
12. Matt 22:1–5, Lk 14:15–24.
13. Rev 2:7.
14. Rev 2:4–5.
15. Jn 15:15, 16:13–14.
16. Matt 10:34–38.
17. Isa 60:1–2.
18. Matt 24:9–13 Because of lawlessness (failure to obey the word) the love (*agape*) of many in the church will grow cold.
19. Rev 13:6–8 The author believes that the new world order is the single system of world government that will give power to the Antichrist and that it will consist of a single monetary, political and religious system. He believes that many Christians will be deceived (because of failure to obey the word) and support this system (Matt 24:9–13).
20. Jn 15:20.
21. Matt 24:11, 2 Pet 2:1–3, 1 Tim 4:1.
22. Jn 10:28.
23. Eph 1:13 (stamp of ownership).
24. Rom 8:18.
25. Rom 8:31.
26. Isa 54:17.
27. Lk 5:39.
28. Matt 25:11–13.
29. Matt 6:31–33.
30. Rev 3:15–22.
31. Jn 2:10.
32. Act 26:12–13.
33. Mal 4:2.
34. Rev 1:16.
35. Jn 8:12.
36. Rev 19:16.
37. Rev 14:14.
38. Rev 1:15, Ezek 1:7.
39. Isa 53:2.
40. 1 Jn 3:2.
41. Jn 1:32.
42. Isa 44:3–4.

43. Jn 7:38.
44. Jn 15:3, Eph 5:26.
45. Eph 1:17–18.
46. 1 Cor 12:1–20.
47. Eph 5:2.
48. 2 Cor 2:14–15.
49. Jn 19:39–42.
50. 2 Cor 2:15–16.
51. Heb 4:12.
52. 2 Cor 2:14–16.
53. Rev 2:26–27.
54. Rev 5:1–14.
55. Eph 1:22–23.
56. Rev 5:10.
57. Dan 2:31–45.
58. Dan 7:14.
59. Isa 61:3.
60. Matt 24:27.
61. Rev 1:5.
62. Rom 8:29.
63. Eph 5:27.
64. 1 Jn 4:17.
65. Jn 14:9.
66. Jam 3:10–12.
67. Prov 18:20–21.
68. Ps 37:30.
69. Lev 19:16, Prov 18:7–8, 1 Tim 5:13.
70. 1 Cor 14:26.
71. Gen 3:1, Jn 10:10.
72. Prov 10:11, 13:14.
73. Prov 18:21.
74. Ps 119:103.
75. 1 Jn 1:5.

76. Jam 1:17.
77. Jam 1:8.
78. Phil 2:5.
79. Lk 6:46.
80. Matt 7:21–23, Jer 9:24.

Song chapter six – pages 67–82

1. Deut 4:29.
2. Rom 10:6–8.
3. Matt 13:24–30, 36–43.
4. 1 Tim 2:4.
5. Mk 16:15.
6. Eccl 4:12.
7. 1 Jn 4:8.
8. Rom 8:35.
9. Act 20:28.
10. Rom 6:17–18, Rev 5:9.
11. 1 Cor 11:23–26.
12. Rev 21:7.
13. Jn 15:7, 1 Jn 5:14–15.
14. Rom 8:17, 32.
15. Num 23:19, Deut 7:9, Ps 89:34.
16. Matt 4:4.
17. Lk 24:44–45.
18. Isa 55:1–3.
19. Eph 6:11–12, 1 Cor 15:57.
20. Col 3:17, Phil 2:9–11.
21. Lev 26:8.
22. Jam 4:7.
23. Col 2:15.
24. 2 Tim 1:7.

25. Josh 1:9.
26. Num 13:30, Josh 1:3.
27. Matt 6:22.
28. 1 Jn 3:2, Rom 8:19.
29. Job 7:17.
30. Ps 8:5 The word translated angels is *Elohiym* which the author believes should be more properly translated God, as it is elsewhere in the Scripture. Gen 1:26 says that man was created in the image of God. The author believes, therefore, that man was created a higher creation than the angels and a little lower than God but in His image. Ps 8:5 says that he was crowned (or encircled) with glory and honour. The author suggests that, as Ps 104:1 says that God was clothed with honour and majesty, man also was clothed in honour and majesty, and when Adam sinned, his covering of glory and honour left him and he realised that he was naked.
31. Rom 8:29, 1 Cor 15:49.
32. Rev 21:2–3.
33. Eph 1:4.
34. Matt 22:14.
35. Esth 2:1–13.
36. Isa 61:3.
37. 1 Pet 3:1–4.
38. Ezek 36:26–27.
39. 2 Cor 5:17.
40. Lk 9:57–62.
41. Eph 5:15–21.
42. Rev 2:4–5.
43. Rev 14:4.
44. Heb 12:2.
45. Rev 22:16.
46. Mal 4:2.
47. Jn 8:12.
48. Rev 21:23.
49 Ps 23:2.
50. Jn 15:5.
51. Gal 5:22–23.
52. Jn 15:8.
53. Rom 12:2.
54. 1 Cor 2:16.
55. Ps 138:8, Phil 2:13.
56. 2 Cor 3:18.
57. Matt 10:8.
58. 1 Jn 2:27.
59. Jn 15:8.
60. Hab 2:14.
61. Heb 1:14.
62. Isa 53:6.
63. Isa 29:13.
64. Jn 15:14–15.
65. Rev 2:4–5.
66. Rev 22:12.
67. Rev 3:20.
68. Matt 5:6.

69. Jn 3:17.
70. 1 Jn 3:8.
71. 2 Cor 10:4.
72. Lk 4 :18–19.
73. Jn 15:5.
74. Phil 2:13.
75. Job 23:14.
76. Ps 37:4 (Delight – means to be soft or pliable).
77. Rom 8:29, 2 Cor 3:18.

Song chapter seven – pages 83–92

1. Rom 10:15.
2. 1 Jn 2:27.
3. Isa 10:27.
4. 1 Jn 3:8.
5. Lk 4:18.
6. Matt 11:28–30.
7. Isa 52:7.
8. Ps 139:13–16.
9. Jn 7:37–39.
10. Jn 19:34.
11. 1 Jn 5:8.
12. Deut 8:3.
13. Rev 20:6.
14. Matt 6:22–23.
15. Matt 23:27–28.
16. 1 Cor 12:10, 1 Jn 4:1.
17. 1 Cor 2:16.
18. 1 Pet 2:9.
19. Rev 22:12 *See* Chapter 1, note 3.

20. 1 Jn 3:2.
21. Ps 8:4.
22. Ezek 28:12.
23. Ps 8:5.
24. Eph 2:6.
25. Ps 40:2.
26. Rev 5:9–14.
27. Rev 4:10.
28. Ps 37:4–6.
29. Matt 21:1–11.
30. Song 2:3.
31. Rom 5:8.
32. Heb 12:2.
33. Eph 1:4–6.
34. Jn 1:12–13.
35. Gen 3:8–9.
36. Gen 1:26.
37. Rev 21:1–7.
38. Jn 4:35, Matt 9:37–38.
39. Jn 15:1–8.
40. Gal 5:22–23.
41. 1 Cor 12:12–18.
42. Matt 13:24–30, 36–43.

Song chapter eight – pages 93–114

1. *See* Chapter 5, note 19.
2. 1 Jn 4:3, 2 Thess 2:3–4.
3. Jn 15:20.
4. Josh 1:9.
5. Matt 24:9–13 *See* Chapter 5, note 18.
6. Deut 31:6,8.

7. Matt 10:32–33.
8. 1 Cor 15:57–58.
9. Zech 4:6, Dan 11:32.
10. Jn 3:1–8.
11. 1 Cor 3:16.
12. 1 Cor 2:11.
13. Phil 1:9–11.
14. 2 Cor 10:5.
15. Ps 91:1–6.
16. Jn 17:20–23.
17. 1 Cor 11:23–26.
18. Rev 19:7–9.
19. Lk 24:44.
20. Rev 2:25.
21. Heb 10:23.
22. Ps 40:2.
23. Matt 7:23.
24. Isa 40:3–5.
25. Ps 46:1.
26. Rev 19:11.
27. Isa 36:6.
28. Mal 3:6, Jam 1:17, Josh 21:45.
29. Isa 11:1–4.
30. Ps 23:4.
31. Jn 1:14.
32. Rom 12:2.
33. Matt 12:33–37.
34. Gen 2:9 and *see* Chapter 2, note 6.
35. Rom 10:17.
36. Rom 10:8–10,13.
37. 1 Pet 1:23, Eph 2:5.
38. Isa 59:16, Ezek 22:30.
39. Gen 1:28, Ps 8:6.
40. Matt 6:8.
41. Isa 49:15–16.
42. Eph 1:13–14.
43. Jer 29:11.
44. 1 Cor 15:54–57.
45. Rev 1:18.
46. Rev 20:14, 21:4.
47. 1 Jn 4:8, Rev 1:8.
48. 1 Jn 5:11.
49. 2 Pet 2:20–22.
50. Jn 6:68.
51. 1 Jn 2:15–17.
52. Gal 5:20–21.
53. Heb 12:15.
54. Matt 24:10–12.
55. 1 Pet 5:8–9, Jam 4:7.
56. Matt 6:14–15.
57. 1 Cor 13:13, 1 Jn 4:8.
58. Jn 13:34–35.
59. Isa 59:19.
60. Matt 19:27–29.
61. Ps 49:7–9.
62. Eph 2:8–9.
63. Heb 12:29.
64. 1 Cor 3:12–15.
65. Mal 3:2–3.
66. Matt 18:3–4.
67. 2 Cor 11:2.
68. 1 Jn 2:15–16.
69. Phil 4:7.
70. Jn 14:27.
71. Phil 4:7.
72. Jer 17:7–8.

73. Jer 29:11.
74. Matt 27:46.
75. Act 2:24.
76. Col 2:2.
77. Rom 8:35.
78. Heb 6:18, Tit 1:2.
79. Heb 13:5.
80. Phil 4:4.
81. Isa 26:3.
82. Matt 20:1.
83. Act 20:28.
84. Matt 13:45–46.
85. 2 Cor 8:9.
86. Heb 1:14, Ps 103:20–21.
87. Gen 1:27.
88. Isa 14:12–15.
89. Eph 2:6.
90. Matt 21:33.
91. Phil 4:19.
92. Matt 6:25–34.
93. Matt 7:7–11.
94. Matt 21:22.
95. Col 1:16.
96. Heb 12:2.
97. 2 Cor 3:5.
98. 1 Tim 5:18.
99. 2 Cor 5:10.
100. Rev 22:17.
101. Gen 1:28, Ps 8:6.
102. Act 1:11.
103. Lk 12:35.
104. Matt 22:2.
105. Rev 19:7–8.
106. 1 Thes 4:16–17.
107. Ps 103:20.
108. Rev 22:20.
109. Rev 22:17.
110. Matt 5:15–16.
111. Matt 22:12, Rev 19:8.
112. 2 Cor 5:21.
113. Lk 21:27–28.
114. Rev 2:7, 11, 17, 26, 3:5, 12, 21.
115. Rom 13:11.
116. Matt 16:3.
117. 1 Thess 5:1.